Yale French Studies

NUMBER 130

Guilty Pleasures: Theater, Piety, and Immorality in Seventeenth- Century France

SPECIAL EDITORS: JOSEPH HARRIS AND JULIA PREST

Yale French Studies

Joseph Harris and Julia Prest, *Special editors for this issue*

Alyson Waters, *Managing editor*

Editorial board: Alice Kaplan (Chair), R. Howard Bloch, Morgane Cadieu, Thomas Connolly, Ian Curtis, Carole Delaitre, Edwin Duval, Thomas Kavanagh, Christopher L. Miller, Maurice Samuels, Christopher Semk

Assistant editor: Robyn G. Pront

Editorial office: 82-90 Wall Street, Room 308

Mailing address: P.O. Box 208251, New Haven, Connecticut 06520-8251

Sales and subscription office:

Yale University Press, P.O. Box 209040

New Haven, Connecticut 06520-0940

Designed by James J. Johnson and set in Trump Medieval Roman by Newgen North America. Printed in the United States of America by Sheridan Books, Michigan.

ISSN 044-0078

ISBN for this issue 978-0-300-22163-3

JOSEPH HARRIS AND JULIA PREST

Editors' Preface: Guilty Pleasures: Theater, Piety, and Immorality in Seventeenth-Century France

Somewhat paradoxically, the seventeenth century has long been re-garded as the heyday both of French theater and of religious and moral anti-theatricalism. Each generation was punctuated by a new moral crisis about the theater—a crisis whose shockwaves long outlasted their original moment. The late 1630s saw a famously intense debate about Corneille's tragicomedy *Le Cid*, with many critics denouncing the scandalous behavior of a Spanish noblewoman prepared to marry her father's killer. Yet while the "querelle du Cid" remained primar-ily an aesthetic debate conducted between literary and cultural fig-ures, three decades later clerics and theologians such as Pierre Nicole and Bernard Lamy entered the fray, questioning the very legitimacy of the theater as an institution; now, aesthetic and ethical debates about individual plays overlapped and intertwined with broader dis-putes about the theater's very right to exist. Finally, in 1694, debates about the theater were once again reawakened when a Theatin monk, Père Caffaro, was forced to formally retract a conciliatory letter to the playwright Edme Boursault in which he argued that the theater was not in itself a corrupt or dangerous institution. Caffaro was com-pelled to do so by no less than Jacques-Bénigne Bossuet, Bishop of Meaux, whose vociferous yet subtle refutation of Caffaro's arguments soon formed the basis for the century's last great anti-theatrical tract, the *Maximes et réflexions sur la comédie*.

Ultimately, the protheatrical lobby won its publicity campaign. In the increasingly secular eighteenth century, seventeenth-century religious critics of the theater were implicitly rejected as outmoded, repressive killjoys who could appreciate neither the value nor the values of France's greatest plays. When Jean-Jacques Rousseau wrote the Enlightenment's landmark anti-theatrical tract, the *Lettre à*

YFS 130, *Guilty Pleasures: Theater, Piety, and Immorality in Seventeenth-Century France*, ed. Harris and Prest, © 2016 by Yale University.

d'Alembert sur les spectacles (1758), he steered resolutely clear of the religious arguments adopted by Bossuet and others in the previous century, and his approach proved influential and enduring. Over the last few decades, however, commentators have started to challenge the received image of early modern religious anti-theatricalists as outmoded, reactionary, and reductive. Gradually, a more critical and less reverential attitude toward "classical" theater has allowed *dix-septiémistes* to take the theories and claims of its opponents more seriously. Indeed, as Jean-Marie Piemme announced back in 1970, it is religious writers who offer some of the period's most incisive and provocative critiques of the practice of spectatorship.[1] Rather than concerning themselves simply with technical issues of poetics, religious anti-theatricalists such as Bossuet, Nicole, and Lamy invariably considered the theater as an institution within its lived context. By grounding dramatic debate in wider reflections about human nature, anti-theatricalist thinkers went far deeper into audience psychology than seventeenth-century mainstream dramatic theory had chosen— or perhaps dared—to do.

PLEASURABLE GUILT?

In comparison with their adversaries, many defenders of the theater often appear strangely unsophisticated in their analysis of human psychology, often retreating behind stock phrases about theater's capacity to blend "pleasure and instruction," but rarely explaining how this process might work. If the protheatrical camp won out in the long run, then, this may well be largely because the object it sought to defend held such an insistent and compelling appeal for the general public regardless of the strength of its adversaries. In this respect, the public's readiness to overlook religious warnings, threats, and arguments and to give in to the theater's more immediate appeals and attractions somewhat proves the anti-theatricalists' point about the power of the dramatic experience.

One of the few things that almost everyone involved in seventeenth-century debates agreed on was that the theater harnesses spectators' capacity for pleasure—and this question of pleasure underpins, either explicitly or tacitly, the articles in this collection. At the same

---

1. Jean-Marie Piemme, "Le théâtre en face de la critique religieuse: un exemple, Pierre Nicole," *XVIIᵉ siècle* 88 (July-September 1970): 49.

time, as this volume also suggests, this apparent consensus about the primary place of pleasure itself masks a variety of different stances. Opinions varied widely about the forms, purposes, moral status, and effects of this pleasure. Protheatrical thinkers made much of theater's capacity to "correct while entertaining,"[2] treating pleasure as the sweetener to make moral lessons more palatable. Anti-theatricalists, however, stressed that whatever pleasure the theater could produce was either itself sinful or at least a source of sin. Most agreed that it could produce pleasure, but blamed this pleasure as both corruptly sensual and able to distract spectators from contemplating whatever implicit moral lessons the work might contain. Some, though, even denied that theater produced real pleasure at all, arguing that it held out empty promises of bringing spectators to "the summit of felicity," only to leave them both glutted and empty at the end of the performance.[3]

This concern with pleasure is offset and complicated throughout this volume by a further issue: that of guilt. Our title, "guilty pleasures," alludes to this crucial discrepancy between theory and practice—between the orthodox anti-theatrical line that held the theater as morally culpable, and the undoubted appeal and popularity of the theater in practice throughout the century. The phrase itself implies pleasures that one knows are forbidden and yet that one gives in to: pleasures, indeed, whose intensity may be increased by their very illicitness. Bossuet hints at this possibility in his refutation of Caffaro; as he argues, when dramatists hope to stoke spectators' passions, "what is licit is off-putting; what is illicit becomes alluring."[4] As Bossuet implies, the fictional world of the theater can represent acts, and enact desires, that would not be permitted in the offstage world, and thereby invite a pleasurably illicit complicity in spectators. Guilt

2. The opening of Molière's first Petition to the King on the topic of *Tartuffe*, "Since the theater's duty is to correct men while diverting them . . . ", is just the most famous seventeenth-century reformulation of Horace's injunction in the *Ars Poetica* that poetry should mix "the pleasing and the instructive." See Molière, "Premier placet au Roi," in *Œuvres completes*, ed. Georges Forestier et al. (Paris: Gallimard [Pléiade], 2010), II, 191, and Horace, *Ars poetica*, in *Classical Literary Criticism*, ed. D. A. Russell and M. Winterbottom (Oxford and New York: Oxford University Press, 1989), 102.
3. Bernard Lamy, *Nouvelles réflexions sur la poétique*, ed. Tony Ghaereert (Paris: Champion, 1997), 182.
4. Jacques-Bénigne Bossuet, *Maximes et réflexions sur la comédie*, in *L'église et le théâtre*, ed. C. Urbain and E. Levesque (Paris: Grasset, 1930), 129.

and culpability are not assigned to spectators' responses post hoc, but have been integral to their pleasures from the very start.

Of course, we cannot nowadays have any direct access to the minds and consciences of everyday seventeenth-century theater spectators and churchgoers, to understand how they might have reconciled, sidestepped, or even savored this inner conflict. Yet a few indiscreet glimpses into the sacrosanct privacy of the confessional suggest that some parishioners, and even practicing playwrights, were concerned about the pleasures that the theater could procure. Indeed, the whole debate that flared up in the 1690s was triggered when the dramatist Boursault expressed some moral qualms about his theatrical vocation to his confessor Caffaro. Attempting to assuage what he calls Boursault's "scrupulous fear" about his conscience, Caffaro wrote him a letter reassuring him that the theater was an essentially innocent recreation, made legitimate by our need for rest and diversion.[5] Drawing on his own experience in the confessional, he reasoned that those parishioners who were wealthy enough to attend the theater displayed no greater propensity to crime or sin than those peasants who were unaware even of the theater's existence.

Bossuet, in turn, harshly dismissed this line of reasoning, implying that since the theater's corrupting pleasures operate on spectators gradually, and even unconsciously, theatergoing parishioners—and by extension their confessors—were particularly ill placed to judge what was happening to them. As Bossuet reasons, the theater effectively suspends spectators' moral and critical faculties so that they are unaware of the corruption that is taking place within them. With its radical notion that the spectator's experience is not a wholly conscious one, Bossuet's intervention reminds us that there can be a vast difference between being "guilty" in the sense of culpable, and feeling "guilty" in the sense of experiencing shame at this culpability.

THEORY AND PRACTICE

The dialogue that this volume pursues, then, is not just one between critics of the theater and its defenders; it also establishes an equally important dialogue between dramatic theory and dramatic practice.

---

5. Père Caffaro, "Lettre d'un théologien illustre par sa qualité et par son mérite," in *L'église et le théâtre*, 68.

After all, as a somewhat chastened Caffaro pertinently (if sheepishly) acknowledged in his official retraction of his letter to Boursault, theory and practice can often be at odds: "Quite often, things are one way in theory but quite different in practice."[6] Modern commentators have rarely taken Caffaro's words here seriously; indeed, many recent studies of moral debates in seventeenth-century theater have focused on dramatic theory to the exclusion of practice. In such studies, individual plays have typically been of interest only insofar as they illustrate more general theoretical principles. We believe that this approach has the unfortunate consequence of establishing a period's theoretical debates as explanatory metadiscourses and thus overlooking how practicing dramatists reflected, engaged with, or entered into these debates through their own plays. In order to redress this imbalance, this volume brings together articles on dramatic theory and articles on dramatic practice, and also explores the various ways in which the two can intersect. One key purpose of this volume is to set dramatic theory and dramatic practice against each other—to illustrate both the gulf that can separate them and their mutual imbrication, with neither providing a stable position from which to comment on the other.

Our first two articles concentrate on works of dramatic criticism and theory, which soon open out into far wider discussions of audience psychology and response. Julia Prest's article focuses on a curious and rich protheatrical piece, the *Lettre sur la comédie de l'Imposteur*, which extrapolates a complex argument about the interrelations of pleasure, reason, virtue, and ridicule in the minds of female spectators from a performance of an early version of Molière's *Tartuffe*. According to the *Lettre*, the reasonable pleasure that female spectators experience at witnessing Panulphe's inappropriate and doomed seduction attempts onstage can pave the way for a powerful response of rejection and mockery to any would-be seducers whom they encounter in real life. Yet while ridiculing and rejecting vice and vicious people might pleasurably bolster one's virtue, anti-theatricalists were often more concerned with spectators' dangerous propensity to seek pleasure by identifying with harmful exemplars onstage. As Joseph Harris argues, while a spectator's capacity to identify with other people and situations is inherent to Lamy's s theory of aesthetic experience, this

6. Père Caffaro, "Réponse du P. Caffaro à Bossuet," in *L'église et le théâtre*, 146.

identification may become problematic in the context of dramatic fictions.

The confusion of self and other we find in identification is not limited to dramatic spectators; it can even threaten the integrity of the writing subject. Whereas both Lamy and the anonymous writer of the *Lettre sur l'Imposteur* present themselves as detached, authoritative commentators on dramatic material, other articles in this collection point to a more complex, intertextual imbrication of theory and practice. As some of these articles suggest, the very act of citing material that one means to criticize can risk compromising or infecting one's own metadiscourse. Sometimes this can be done knowingly, and to deliberate comic effect. As Michael Call points out here, for example, Molière's critics often exploit elements of Molière's own dramaturgy—the supposed obscenity of the notorious "le" in *L'école des femmes*, or the metatheatrical framework of *La critique de l'École des femmes*—and thus capitalize on the very processes they hope to condemn or debunk. This corruption can sometimes be still more troubling. Emilia Wilton-Godberfforde's article shows how anti-theatrical religious writing can itself become corrupted by contact with the works it means to condemn. As she explains, not only do writers like Nicole expose their own readers to harm by citing lengthy excerpts from the very works they denounce, but their own anti-theatrical writings also gravitate toward tropes of concealment, unveiling, and resolution that curiously echo techniques used by dramatists.

Yet it is not only theoretical metadiscourses that can become textually corrupted by contact with their objects. Rather, as some of the contributors here suggest, plays can also thematize theoretical concerns. Far from being passive objects of theoretical analysis and dissection, comedies and tragedies themselves can sometimes offer astute, if indirect, comments on the concerns of dramatic theory. This is most clearly the case in explicitly metatheatrical plays. Call's article, for example, reads both Molière's *L'école des femmes* and its metatheatrical sequel *La critique de l'École des femmes* as engaging with a common thematic concern: that of pleasure. Hall Bjørnstad also explores the complex power relations of audience pleasure in his provocative reading of Rotrou's metatheatrical religious tragedy *Le véritable Saint-Genest*. Shifting critical attention away from Genest the actor to the emperor Dioclétian, the play within a play's principal spectator, Bjørnstad traces the masochistic nature of Dioclétian's submission to Genest's performance and the pleasurable "confusion" it arouses in him.

That said, plays do not have to be explicitly metatheatrical to engage with the moral issues of dramatic debate, as Nicholas Hammond's article suggests. Seizing on the proliferation of tropes of poison in and around Racine's theater, Hammond shows how Racine's last secular tragedy *Phèdre* can be read as a complex and indirect commentary on the debate about dramatic morality originally triggered by Nicole's description of playwrights as "public poisoners." As Hammond points out, Racine's own withdrawal from the stage after *Phèdre* symbolically mirrors the suicide by poison of his last secular heroine.

The next two articles also support Hammond's suggestion that plays are not always just passive objects of theoretical scrutiny, but can also become potent interventions in wider debates. In different ways, Perry Gethner and Theresa Kennedy show how religious dramatists attempted to harness the power of the theater for an appropriate moral effect. One way in which dramatists responded to moral criticism involved attempting to purge their theater of those elements that had been flagged as most harmful, not least by removing those love plots apparently able to stoke passionate concupiscence in spectators. Gethner's article, conversely, homes in on a few problematic cases when dramatists included love plots in biblical tragedies, sometimes even inventing love plots absent from the biblical source. These plots suggest the conviction of playwrights such as Du Ryer and Boyer that even such unstable and dangerous subject matter as illicit passion can, in the right hands, be harnessed to apparently positive moral effect. An important figure in both articles is Louis XIV's second wife, Madame de Maintenon, who drew on theatrical techniques as a tool of moral instruction in her girls' school at Saint-Cyr. Kennedy explores how Maintenon devised new dramatic modes, such as proverbs and conversations, in an attempt to instill her young charges with moral values. As Kennedy makes clear, however, Maintenon might have found new ways to use theatrical modes for moral instruction, and of course this moral instruction was essentially conservative, encouraging young women—and noblewomen at that—to adopt lives of domestic servitude.

Our final two articles move from theatrical performance within convents and girls' schools to ecclesiastical practice and ritual. In 1688 La Bruyère lamented the fact that sermons had become "a spectacle" and "one sort of entertainment among a thousand others."[7] Similarly, the articles by Christopher Semk and Fabien Cavaillé here explore different ways in which theatrical paradigms threatened to taint Church practice and ritual, at least from the perspective of the parishioner. Semk's article explores the fraught question of pleasure that underpinned—but also threatened to undermine—religious oratory. As Semk suggests, experience of the theater can lead to a "theatricalizing" or "aestheticizing" stance toward religious ceremony that can affect the congregants' reception of sermons. Cavaillé's article traces comparable anxieties, arguing that the recurrent alimentary images that Nicole uses in his critiques of the theater testify to an anxiety about bodily consumption that threatens the very status of the Eucharist. Both articles stress the bodiliness of congregational practices—the stimulation of the ear during sermons, or the digestive process of consuming the Host. Like going to the theater, eating food and listening to pleasant sermons are both sensory, even sensual, experiences.

CONCLUSION

Even today, Western theater cannot fully shake off its association with the notion of guilty pleasure, although the emphasis now is not so much on any fear of moral corruption during or following a performance as on, at one end of the spectrum, the embarrassment of admitting to appreciating lighter, more lowbrow theatrical genres and, at the other, the discomfort of appreciating the work of someone whose personal views we do not share or even find abhorrent. For many, fans of Wagner opera are inherently guilty by association owing to the composer's notoriously anti-Semitic views, and their enjoyment of a performance of a Wagner opera thus becomes a guilty pleasure. Mostly, however, the debate over mainstream, Western theater in the twenty-first century is an aesthetic one: we want to know if a new work or production is any good, not if we are likely to be corrupted by it. It is, rather, in the context of film that some of the debates discussed in this volume reappear; after all, cinema can present seemingly realistic portrayals of, in particular, sex and violence of an intimacy and intensity that are still unthinkable on the live

---

7. Jean de La Bruyère, *Les caractères de Théophraste traduits du grec, avec les caractères ou mœurs de ce siècle* (Paris: Champion, 1999), 559.

stage. But the issues explored here resonate most strikingly with on-going discussions in another arena: new technologies and particularly the internet. Were the seventeenth-century anti-theatricalists alive today, there is little doubt that they would be addressing matters relating to cyberethics. Indeed, the notion of "virtual morality" is the modern cousin of the theatrical morality that seventeenth-century playwrights claimed to seek and that their fiercest critics deemed an impossibility.

JULIA PREST

Failed Seductions and the Female Spectator: Pleasure and Polemic in the *Lettre sur la comédie de l'Imposteur*

One of the most common charges leveled against the theater in seventeenth-century France was that it promoted immorality in general and sexual immorality in particular. While the Church sought to suppress dangerous passions and whims, it was claimed that the theater, owing in part to its preoccupation with erotic love, enflamed them. René Rapin, a Jesuit, attributed the increasing emphasis on *galanterie* (a broad term encompassing anything from mild flirtation to extramarital sexual relations) in seventeenth-century drama precisely to the increasing and unwelcome influence of the female spectator.[1] Likewise, Pierre Nicole, a Jansenist, outlined the process by which the inclusion of *galanterie* in plays and novels insidiously undermined society by indulging women's unrealizable fantasies.[2] For Nicole and others, the theatrical (and novelistic) portrayal of *galanterie* thus threatened to compromise the sacrament of marriage through the vector of the impressionable female.

One of the most intriguing elements of the anonymous *Lettre sur la comédie de l'Imposteur* (1667) lies in its response to this very charge. The author of the *Lettre* makes the extraordinary claim that Molière's *Tartuffe, ou l'hypocrite*, now renamed *Panulphe, ou l'imposteur*, offers a powerful attack on, and a reliable inoculation against, *galanterie solide* (a euphemism for fornication). The argument hinges on an intriguing theory of ridicule: the author claims that the effect of seeing Panulphe-Tartuffe's attempted seduction of

1. See René Rapin, *Réflexions sur la poétique d'Aristote et sur les ouvrages des poètes anciens et modernes* (Paris: Muguet, 1674), 183–84.
2. *Traité de la comédie* (1667), ed. Georges Couton (Paris: Belles Lettres, 1961), 61–62.

YFS 130, *Guilty Pleasures: Theater, Piety, and Immorality in Seventeenth-Century France*, ed. Harris and Prest, © 2016 by Yale University.

La Dame-Elmire is so powerful that the extreme sense of ridicule it engenders among the theater audience is indelible and will inevitably be called to mind in any similar off-stage encounters. The play, it is argued, is thus endowed with a significant moral function that can only benefit the French nation currently experiencing a tide of sexual immorality. The argument put forward is intriguing, yet slippery in its moral ambiguity and sometimes obfuscatory logic. Here I will attempt to unpack these claims, paying particular attention to the emphasis placed on the response of the female spectator and the author's identification with her. I shall also speculate on the author's purpose in writing this portion of the letter and what contribution it might have made in the context of the *Tartuffe* controversy.

As all *moliéristes* know, *Tartuffe, ou l'hypocrite* was banned from public performance immediately following its courtly première at Versailles on May 12, 1664. This marked the beginning of a controversy that would last nearly five years during which time Molière battled to have the ban lifted and the young Louis XIV sought to establish himself as king and to ensure religious and political stability within his kingdom.[3] The *Lettre*, dated August 20, 1667, appeared with no indication of the name of the author, the place of publication, or the name of the printer, and it seems to have been circulated covertly.[4] Although the identity of its author is unknown, it seems clear from the form, tone, and content of the letter that it was written by a member of the circle of free-thinking intellectuals that Molière frequented.[5] The letter's appearance followed in the wake of a single public performance at the Palais-Royal theater of *Panulphe, ou l'imposteur* on August 5, 1667, which had sparked the immediate renewal and reinvigoration of a controversy that was still simmering. On August 6, Guillaume Lamoignon, first president of the Paris *Parlement*, intervened in the king's absence and put a stop to any further performances of the play, and Molière's attempts in the days that followed

---

3. For a full discussion of the controversy, see Julia Prest, *Controversy in French Drama: Molière's* Tartuffe *and the Struggle for Influence* (New York: Palgrave, 2014).

4. See La Mothe Le Vayer, *Lettre sur la comédie de l'Imposteur*, ed. Robert McBride (Durham: University of Durham, 1994), Durham Modern Languages Series FT4, 49. All parenthetical page references to the letter in the present article are to this edition.

5. McBride attributes the *Lettre* to Molière's friend, François de La Mothe Le Vayer (1588–1672). Scholars have been slow to accept this attribution, however, and other names that are commonly put forward are Jean Donneau de Visé and Claude-Emmanuel Huillier, better known as Chapelle.

to change Lamoignon's mind were unsuccessful. Nor did the play-wright's (second) petition to the king, written on August 8 and delivered to the monarch in his military camp in Lille shortly thereafter, have any immediate effect. The most powerful assault on the play came on August 11, 1667, in the form of Archbishop Péréfixe's extraordinarily heavy-handed decree that threatened excommunication to anybody within his diocese who performed, read, or heard the play.

The body of the *Lettre*, an epistolary fiction, opens with an allusion to this decree, ironically observing that the writer has committed a crime by seeing the play and indicating that he can be forgiven only if he brings his fictional addressee up to speed on what the latter has missed. If the letter is ostensibly addressed to one "Monsieur," it is in fact addressed to anybody who was not present at the sole public performance on August 5. Among other things, then, the *Lettre sur la comédie de l'Imposteur* seeks to subvert Péréfixe's ban, for its first and longest part includes a detailed scene by scene account of the 1667 version of the play, in which the verse script is closely paraphrased in prose (usually through reported speech), but never quite openly cited. This account is allegedly based on the author's memory of the performance, although this is a manifestly disingenuous claim for the level of detail and accuracy indicate that the author had access to a copy of the play, which in turn suggests that it was written, or at least conceived, with the playwright's consent. Indeed, the principal value of the *Lettre* is often thought by modern critics to lie in the fact that it provides the nearest thing available to a text that is no longer extant. The *Lettre* is also recognized for its vigorous and sometimes quirky defense of the inclusion of religious subject matter in the theater, an objection that Lamoignon had reportedly raised with Molière when they met in August 1667 and which we are told had caught the playwright off guard.[6] To an extent, then, the *Lettre* may be understood to have offered a prompt response both to the new ban and to the latest argument put forward against the play.

The argument regarding religion and theater might conceivably have been intended to convince those who shared Lamoignon's view of the benefits of bringing religion to the world, though this seems highly unlikely for reasons that are outlined below. Meanwhile, the scene by scene account of the play is clearly intended to provoke those

---

6. See *Correspondance entre Boileau Despréaux et Brossette*, ed. Auguste Laverdet (Paris: Techener, 1858), 564–65 for an account of the meeting.

who shared Péréfixe's objections: it is packed full of value-judgments and personal commentaries with regard to the moral excellence, for instance, of the Cléante figure who, as I have discussed elsewhere, is no orthodox Christian.[7] The author addresses the question of any polemical intent with some irony as he moves from the first part of the letter into the second. He writes that he will not engage with the play as religious polemic, claiming that such delicate matters are not for him. Yet he also makes the passing and indubitably controversial assertion, grounded in his firm belief in the external ridiculousness of *all* forms of falsehood, that true and false devotion, like all cases of true and false, *are* thereby distinguishable. Rather than engage (further) in this sticky debate, the author proposes instead to offer two reflections that, he claims, do not relate to the substance of the controversy.

However, his extensive engagement with the question of fornication and adultery is surely more provocative than it is mollifying.[8] The most incendiary dimension to the *Lettre* (and the most likely reason for its anonymity), though, lies in its openly, shockingly even, unorthodox view of religion and in its secular, philosophical outlook, which is broadly that of the erudite libertine. The author writes with great authority and assurance that religion is nothing more than the perfection of reason (94); he also comments on the strange power that religion has over men's minds (78). Unequivocal in its rejection of orthodox religion, the letter is couched in terms of a moral philosophy that is materialist and empirical, shot through with a strong epicurean bent. The moral perspective that is put forward in the letter is thoroughly secular, and as such is incompatible with the Christian religion. As Jean-Pierre Cavaillé has noted, the type of truth that is promoted here is not the divinely revealed truth enjoyed by the faithful Christian but the unqualified truth associated with human reason.[9]

---

7. See "Where are the *vrais dévots* and are they *véritables gens de bien*? Eloquent Slippage in the *Tartuffe* Controversy," *Neophilologus* 96/3 (2012) [online version] or 97/2 (2013): 283–97 [print version].

8. There is reason to believe that the scenes in which Panulphe-Tartuffe attempts to seduce La Dame-Elmire were also considered objectionable to Molière's detractors. See Prest, "Elmire and the Erotics of the Ménage à Trois in Molière's *Tartuffe*," *Romanic Review* 102 (2011): 129–44.

9. Jean-Pierre Cavaillé, "Hypocrisie et Imposture dans la querelle du *Tartuffe* (1664–1669): La *Lettre sur la comédie de l'Imposteur* (1667)," *Les Dossiers du Grihl*. http://dossiersgrihl.revues.org/292; DOI: 10.4000/dossiersgrihl.292, paragraph 33.

For the author, there is no need for any type of divine intervention in matters of truth since man has been given all the tools he needs to identify it through natural reason; there is no place for a divine or religious source of morality.

In the Church's eyes, this is an unequivocally and profoundly libertine text, and indeed it cannot credibly have been written with the aim of winning over Molière's devout detractors. Rather, the letter's argumentation stems from an entirely different worldview and is predicated on the tacit assumption that its readers will share the author's moral outlook. We may conclude that if the author intended to make any contribution to the polemic at all, it was in the form of a provocative riposte rather than a persuasive counter-argument, a means to stir up controversy (or at least to rail against its absurdity with likeminded individuals) rather than to appease it.

The first part of the *Lettre* is, as we have seen, given over to a detailed summary of the play. The second part is dedicated broadly to a defense of the play's morality, firstly by means of a justification of the inclusion of religion in the theater and secondly by a detailed account of Molière's alleged assault on sexual immorality. The intricate theory of laughter and the ridiculous put forward in this final section of the letter has caught the attention of a number of modern critics. It has usefully been likened in its reliance on a sense of superiority and pride to the theory put forward by Hobbes in his *Treatise on Human Nature* (1650) and in *Leviathan* (1651), and in its emphasis on *disconvenance* (unsuitability) and on social correction to the theory Henri Bergson set out more recently in *Le rire* (1900). However, insufficient attention has been paid to his extraordinary claims specifically in relation to *galanterie* via which this theory is put forward, and with which we are principally concerned here.

Given its intricate, sinuous, and sometimes elusive nature, the anonymous author's argument will be examined here in detail. The argument is presented in the letter's opening foreword as being too speculative and still five or six months away from completion (71). The author, writing of himself in the third person, explains that he will outline a happy byproduct of viewing the play that he believes can be put to good use in the fight against *galanterie* and would-be male seducers (72). There is no suggestion, then, that Molière actively sought to enter the campaign against sexual immorality, but rather that this is an accidental benefit of his play. The author then goes on to present his startling claim whereby the play represents the most significant contribution to the campaign to preserve marital fidelity thanks to its ridiculous portrayal of the most common methods employed by would-be seducers (97). If modern readers are surprised by this argument, it would seem that we are not alone, for the author readily admits that some readers will find the proposition strange, but he asks them to suspend their judgment until they too have seen the play (97). Anticipating the counter-argument whereby *galanterie* is the most natural of all vices and therefore almost impossible to counter, the author admits that it is indeed the most universal of sins but claims that this is owing not to an inherent predisposition among all humans but rather to the peculiarities of the French nation, especially its women (97). On the basis of the culturally constructed nature of French women's inclination toward *galanterie*, the author argues that the extreme ridicule with which the encounters and arguments that usually serve as preludes to illicit sexual liaisons are treated in the play will ably serve to counteract the charms that lead most women astray (97).

According to the author's theory of ridicule, nature has endowed reason with qualities that help us to identify that reason, notably a sense of joy and of pleasure that our soul finds in all forms of morality. This is distinct from the type of pleasure that we derive from something that is not reasonable and which, for its part, provokes our capacity to perceive something as being ridiculous (98). Reason is thus associated with a form of joy that is mixed with esteem, whereas unreason (and ridicule) is associated with one that is mixed with scorn. Reason is associated with *convenance* (suitability or compatibility) and *bienséance* (propriety), while unreason and ridicule are evidenced by *disconvenance* (unsuitability or incompatibility). Ridicule is nature's way of telling us to avoid something and, the author observes, if incompatibility is the essence of ridicule then it is easy to see how Panulphe's attempted seduction, like all forms of hypocrisy, is ridiculous because the secret behavior of such bigots does not correspond with their public image (98). Panulphe-Tartuffe is thus ridiculous firstly because he is a hypocrite.

Panulphe's attempted seduction, we are told, is doubly ridiculous because it is unsuccessful. When we see that Panulphe fails to convince Elmire, we conclude that the means he uses are grossly at odds with the outcome, and that consequently he is ridiculous for having used those means in the first place. And because both Panulphe's austerity and his attempts at seducing Elmire are extreme, he is consequently extremely ridiculous (99). This extremity is key to the matter of transferability, which the author then addresses, rightly anticipating the problematic question of how the special case of Panulphe, who is a man of religion, would subsequently apply to men of the world. The author explains that the extremity of Panulphe's amorous attempts is such that when similar events occur at any time and in any context in the future they will remain ridiculous to the former spectator of the play, even if their impact is slightly lessened (99). It is owing to the soul's inclination toward pleasure that it will seek to reactivate the sense of pleasure that it experienced the first time around even if the circumstances are somewhat different. The hypothetical example is given of a woman who, when under pressure from a man using the same arguments that Panulphe had used, inevitably finding them ridiculous, will fail to reflect upon the differences between the man in front of her and Panulphe (99–100). In this instance, her capacity for reason will be overridden by her soul's inclination toward the pleasure of extreme ridicule. This confusion of two different instances of attempted seduction, one theatrical, the other real, one couched in religious terms, the other in worldly ones, is owing to the operations of memory and especially of the imagination, which, according to our author, is the natural home of ridicule (100). This erratic behavior in the human soul, the author argues, is the necessary consequence of the violent and strong impression that the phenomenon made the first time around.

With particular reference to Panulphe's arguments, the author explains that because they failed spectacularly in Molière's play, they will necessarily also fail offstage when presented to a woman who has seen the play. And even a more modest sense of ridicule recalled will have the benefit of buying the woman under attack some more time before she realizes that her *galant* and Panulphe are not in fact one and the same (100). The early moments of an attempted seduction are crucial, we are told, and a sense of ridicule is the ultimate passion killer (101); indeed, for the individual who is the object of ridicule, the male seducer, it is the most shocking, the most repellent, and the most odious of all sentiments. This is the case for all objects of ridicule but particularly so for the male lover. The author explains that this stems from the fact that there is nothing more pleasing than arousing passion in another and therefore nothing more displeasing than the coldness and apathy provoked by ridicule. The effect of the woman's cold response is to dampen the ardor or at least the effectiveness of the man's passion (102).

The author then goes on to make the fascinating claim that *all* such amorous declarations are ridiculous since any external appearances that differ from the internal substance are essentially ridiculous. All would-be seducers are dissembling hypocrites because no man would want to admit in public the feelings that he would describe in private to a woman whom he wanted to seduce (102). For our author, the *galant* who states anything other than that his goal is his own sexual gratification is necessarily a hypocrite.

Toward the end of the letter, the author seeks to drive his point home by insisting on the ubiquity of the problem of sexual immorality and of the uniquely superior nature of Molière's contribution to the fight against it. He observes that the current state of affairs is a result of a popular misconception with regard to sexual mores according to which religion directly contradicts natural reason (104). The author, it is implied, differs from many *mondains* in considering adultery to be a pressing moral issue; however, as we have seen, his morality is not strictly Christian. Similarly, we note that the logic of his argument here depends on the assumed prioritization of natural reason over religion; and reason, applied via the effects of Molière's play, will succeed where religion and other more conventional methods of attempting to police sexual morality continually fail (104). In an ironic rhetorical flourish, the author notes finally that in pointing all this out he is in fact doing Molière a great disservice, because he is creating enemies for him in the shape and form of all the *galants* in Paris.

What are we to make of these claims? According to one critic, the argument is so extraordinary that it has not reappeared since.[10] Yet this line of reasoning, for all its extravagance, is difficult to dismiss, not least because it is so obviously the product of an intelligent and interesting mind. And the notion of laughter as a useful corrective tool enjoyed considerable currency in the seventeenth century and beyond. Molière himself had invoked the idea for the first time in his first petition to Louis XIV, written in August 1664, in which he stated that comedy's moral function was to correct men while entertaining

10. Herman Prins Salomon, *Tartuffe devant l'opinion française* (Paris: PUF, 1962), 62.

them, and he was to return to the idea in his Preface to the published edition of *Tartuffe* in 1669, when he observed that men can easily bear to be reprimanded but cannot stand being mocked. However, the particular vice that Molière was claiming to correct in his *Tartuffe* was of course hypocrisy, and there is no mention by the playwright of any possible benefit with relation to *galanterie*. It is the application of the principle of laughter as a moral corrective to the question of sexual immorality that is particularly surprising in our *Lettre*.

The notion that the inopportune lover is a ridiculous figure was widely accepted; it is a comic trope and one that features repeatedly in Molière's drama. The particular absurdity of the old man chasing after a much younger woman—a theme dear to Molière—would even be drawn on by Bossuet in his attempts to ensure that Louis XIV would henceforth remain on the straight and narrow. In his Easter sermon for 1681, Bossuet warned Louis XIV that any sexual exploits in kingly old age would make him an object of ridicule, but would not enable his conversion.[11] The other great preacher of the age, Bourdaloue, likewise imputes a corrective purpose to laughter when he comments that any mockery of his devotion will either result in useful self-correction or, if unjustified, fall on deaf ears.[12] While this too is woefully inadequate when the stakes are eternal salvation or damnation, in the context of a moral philosophy that is unconcerned with the afterlife, the effectiveness of laughter in the here and now might reasonably be proclaimed to be of significant moral benefit to society.

The more problematic aspect of the argument put forward in the *Lettre* lies with the question of transferability and the crucial role played by laughter in that process. The difficulty sits not with the idea that what is seen onstage might subsequently be applied to events offstage, for this was commonly understood by people on both sides of the theatrical debate. Rather it is to be found in the idea that the particular case of Panulphe-Tartuffe's attempted seduction of La Dame-Elmire in a theatrical fiction would be applied to *all* attempted seductions encountered thereafter offstage, even if they occurred in an entirely different social context. The author is of course aware of this problem and the intricacy (and one might say obfuscation) of his

11. Cited in Georges Couton, *La chair et l'âme: Louis XIV entre ses maîtresses et Bossuet* (Grenoble: Presses Universitaires de Grenoble, 1995), 178.
12. *Œuvres complètes de Bourdaloue*, ed. Prêtres de l'Immaculée-Conception de Saint-Dizier, 4 vols (Bar-le-Duc/Paris: Guérin, 1864), IV: 362.

argumentation (particularly with regard to the operation of the imagination) is clearly an attempt to render a shaky claim at least more rhetorically convincing. But the argument's rhetorical intricacy is also its downfall, for at the same time that the reader is impressed by the rhetorical skill with which it is presented, s/he is left to question its actual logic. And while the author anticipates a number of queries, these are of course selective and many questions remain unanswered.

The pleasure that an individual takes in his or, in this case, her experience of another's ridicule, for instance, is problematic both because it is founded on a sense of personal pride and superiority vis-à-vis the other, which is morally dubious, and particularly because it is in conflict with nature's supposed impulse toward what is morally good, which in turn produces another, purer form of pleasure. Why is the soul so reluctant to let go of the pleasure of ridicule when so many other potential pleasures are available? How exactly is one to explain the fact that the pleasurable experience of another's ridicule produces a marked coldness toward the individual in question? And can the author convincingly claim that a drive toward illicit sexual encounters is more a product of French female culture than a natural impulse? These are only some of the many queries that an attentive reader of the *Lettre* might raise.

The notion of transferability is particularly problematic in the context of the *Tartuffe* controversy given that the principal complaint made about the play was precisely that the memory of Tartuffe-Panulphe would subsequently taint the impression made by off-stage *dévots*. Only a few days before the *Lettre* appeared, Archbishop Péréfixe had stated in his famous decree that the play was:

> all the more likely to cause harm to religion owing to the fact that, while claiming to condemn hypocrisy or false devotion, [it] provides grounds to accuse indiscriminately all those who profess the most steadfast piety and thereby exposes them to the continual mockery and slander of the libertines.[13]

Some years later, one Coustel would neatly spell out the process:

> On the pretext of condemning false devotion, Molière represents his Tartuffe's wickedness with such intensity and has him pronounce such repugnant teachings that the corruption of the human heart will

13. In Molière, *Œuvres complètes*, ed. Georges Forestier and Claude Bourqui et al, 2 vols, Pléiade (Paris: Gallimard, 2010) II: 1168. My translation.

not fail to apply these not to a Tartuffe in the theater but to a real-life man of religion.[14]

Péréfixe's allegation does hint at the dissuasive power of ridicule, while Coustel's account of the extremity of Tartuffe's portrayal is the humorless negative image of the extreme ridicule described in the *Lettre*. Both Coustel and our anonymous author agree that the theatrical Tartuffe-Panulphe is an extreme case and that he will leave a powerful impression in the mind of the spectator that will subsequently be brought to bear on real-life experiences. But they diverge wildly on the effects of this application, which are profoundly pernicious for Coustel and morally beneficial for our anonymous author. To turn transferability on its head and apply it to something other than religion is a clever tour de force on the part of the author of the *Lettre*, but not one that can have seriously sought to change the mind of Péréfixe or even Lamoignon. Indeed the author's generalized summary of the process is indistinguishable from the very basis on which vociferous complaints about the play were made: "We shall be unable to take seriously those things that we have already perceived as ridiculous or which bear some relation to a former sense of ridicule of which we are subsequently reminded" (101).

For this and all the other reasons outlined above, we are obliged to look beyond actual persuasion as the *raison d'être* of this letter. The evident relish with which it was written offers an important clue to its purpose, as does the insistence on pleasure as a driving force in human behavior, be it the scornful pleasure to be derived from another's ridicule or the esteem-filled pleasure of encountering what is good and reasonable. A further clue is found in the author's attitude toward his own thesis as he expresses it near the end of the letter. Anticipating the objection whereby the spectator's response might not in fact be exactly as he has described, the author admits that it is notoriously difficult even for the person in question to know what his or her response to something really is, and that the most reliable gauge of truth is the type of logical reasoning that he has applied to the matter throughout. Proof, he concludes, is provided by insight and the power of reasoning. The pleasure of reading and of writing this part of the text lies precisely with its intricate, seemingly logical argumentation, which can be enjoyed and admired even as it is dis-

14. *Sentimens de l'Eglise & des SS. Peres pour servir de discussion sur la Comedie et les comediens* (Paris: Coignard, 1694), 66. My translation.

puted. This is a text, then, that is driven to a large extent by aesthetic and rhetorical pleasure.

The author's particular interest in audience response is surely one of the most interesting and pleasurable elements of the letter. If audience response is, as the author admits, notoriously difficult to pin down at the best of times, he creates an additional challenge for himself by giving so much weight specifically to the response of the female spectator.[15] Although the author claims that only individuals who have seen the play are equipped to comment on its effects, he does not at any point in his discussion of *galanterie* offer a personal response to the question grounded in experience. More surprising still is the fact that he does not at any point indicate what the unmediated response of the generic *male* spectator might be to Panulphe-Tartuffe's attempted seduction. A simpler and perhaps more convincing argument in favor of the benefits of ridiculous *galanterie* would have been to claim that would-be male seducers in Molière's audience would identify sufficiently with Panulphe-Tartuffe's techniques (if not with his person) to have a foretaste of their own ridiculousness in a similar situation in the future and thereby to undergo some inoculation against their own ridicule. Instead, the author of the *Lettre* has the male seducer experience his own ridiculousness only via the perception and subsequent coldness of the erstwhile female spectator. Only then will he feel an appropriate sense of shame or hesitancy with regard to his actions. According to this model, the supposedly beneficial effects of ridicule do not operate directly on the male audience at all; indeed, the male seducer need not have seen *L'imposteur* at all in order to feel its effects. It is only the female spectator who puts the theory into effect.

To what extent, then, can this argument be considered proto-feminist? French women are portrayed by the author as being in the grip of a social pressure to commit adultery and are seen as the (sometimes willing) victims of the machinations of the male adulterers around them. They are thus complicit in their adultery, but they are not its prime instigators. It is the men who are corrupting (*les corrupteurs*), and the women who are the victims (*les attaquées*). There is no suggestion in the *Lettre* that women are lascivious temptresses bent, Eve-like, upon leading men astray; indeed, this misogynist outlook is

---

15. While it is not impossible that the *Lettre* might have been written by a woman, my argument is based on the assumption that its author was male.

antithetical to the whole tenor of the letter. And the fact that responsibility for preventing fornication—as well as, crucially, the means to do so—is passed by the author to the female sex may be understood as promoting a considerable degree of female empowerment, even if it is achieved involuntarily by means of an active imagination. As we have seen, according to the logic of the author's argument, the female spectator will, upon encountering a man intent on leading her astray, enjoy anew the pleasure of Panulphe-Tartuffe's ridiculousness and thereby find herself sufficiently well armed to resist her *galant*'s advances. That she should want ultimately to resist is predicated on the twin assumptions that adultery is to be avoided and that it does more harm to a woman's reputation than to a man's. The first point is owing not to the fact that adultery is prohibited in the Bible, but because it is a product of unreason; likewise, the second point appears to derive not from a widespread wish to control female behavior but instead from a straightforward and sympathetic, even empathetic, understanding of the female predicament. The mental cross-dressing required by the author's emphasis on the female response also represents a welcome means to develop and display his own rhetorical prowess as well as his imaginative skill. The author's pleasure in writing his text, like ours in reading it, lies ultimately in the construction of an intricate and intriguing argument that is articulately made.

Are we to conclude that the letter prioritizes pleasure over polemic? While the pleasurable dimension to the letter's virtuosity is undeniable, the nature of its polemical contribution is perhaps not so immediately apparent. Indeed, the letter appears to have had no discernible effect whatsoever on the outcome of the *Tartuffe* controversy, and there is no evidence to suggest that it ever sincerely sought to do so. In that sense, the *Lettre*'s contribution to the *Tartuffe* controversy is above all circumstantial. Rather than attempting to change the minds of the anti-Tartuffians, the letter sought firstly to subvert their influence by circulating a detailed summary of a play that was banned, and secondly to contradict their opinions by means of arguments grounded in a moral philosophy that was antithetical to orthodox religion but quietly shared by an increasing number of individuals. And to ascribe a moral purpose to the theater on the basis of secular precepts that allow considerable scope for pleasure was of course highly provocative.

If we are ultimately unconvinced by the practical, moral application of the ridicule of Panulphe's failed seduction of La Dame, the secularized female spectator of the *Lettre* is today a more compelling and familiar figure than the dangerously weak (but powerfully tempting) female portrayed by Nicole and other anti-theatricalists. The playful, ludic nature of the argument similarly represents a challenge to the serious tone usually adopted by the religiously motivated writers of 1660s France. In this way, different types of pleasure—rhetorical, aesthetic, and moral, as well as the very pleasure of polemic—are put into the service of a polemic that extends far beyond the immediate concerns of the *Tartuffe* controversy. For the letter's bold (re)secularization of a theatrical controversy that had become embroiled in a religious polemic is of a more general and far-reaching nature, and one that hints at the radical changes in worldview that would eventually lead to the end of the ancien régime itself.

JOSEPH HARRIS

Playing with Fire? Bernard Lamy and the Pleasures of Identification

It is surely no coincidence that the 1660s, the decade that saw the first of the seventeenth century's two major moments of sustained religious anti-theatrical discourse, also reveal a more general shift in the understanding of dramatic spectatorship. Two issues above all started to take on a particular prominence in mid-century dramatic debates. Firstly, discussions of dramatic pleasure started to shift in emphasis; earlier debates about whether theater's primary goal was to "please" or to "instruct" gave way to more complex—if still somewhat tentative—attempts to establish what the nature of this dramatic pleasure might actually be. Secondly, the essentially perceptual and cognitive questions of dramatic illusion that had previously dominated dramatic thought gave way to more intersubjective concerns about spectators' affective, emotional relationship to onstage characters putatively deemed real.[1] One of the most striking manifestations of this newly theorized emotional bond between audience and characters involves what we might nowadays call "identification." Many recent commentators have been quick to label these psychological processes as identificatory; for example, Laurent Thirouin has insisted that "classical" French is essentially incapable of referring to any "intellectual complicity . . . that does not involve a full identification."[2] Seventeenth-century thinkers sometimes interpret these identificatory processes in quite different ways. Pro-theatrical writers, for ex-

1. I discuss these two movements in my *Inventing the Spectator: Subjectivity and the Theatrical Experience in Early Modern France* (Oxford: Oxford University Press, 2014), especially in chapters 4 and 6.
2. Laurent Thirouin, *L'aveuglement salutaire: Le réquisitoire contre le théâtre dans la France classique* (Paris: Champion, 2007), 124. All translations in this essay are my own.

YFS 130, *Guilty Pleasures: Theater, Piety, and Immorality in Seventeenth-Century France,* ed. Harris and Prest, © 2016 by Yale University.

ample, typically present identification in relatively indirect terms. In one of the period's dominant readings of catharsis, for example, the spectator first constructs an analogy between himself and the tragic hero based on shared character traits, and then—in a crucial subsequent moment of dis-identification or disengagement—purges himself of any dangerous overlap of temperament or passion with the suffering character. This theory is summed up neatly by Corneille in his "Discours de la tragédie":

> Our pity for misfortune which we see befalling our likes leads us to fear something similar for ourselves; this fear leads to the desire to avoid it; and this desire leads us to purge, moderate, rectify, and even uproot from ourselves the passion that we see plunging those we lament into misfortune, for the common but natural and certain reason that to avoid the effect we must remove the cause.[3]

It is perhaps unsurprising that defenders of the theater should be keen to downplay identification's potentially troubling irrationality by subordinating it to a discourse of "natural" reason and logic. In contrast, anti-theatricalists such as Nicole, Conti, and later Bossuet tend to offer far subtler and more incisive accounts of spectator response than their opponents' somewhat perfunctory claims about purgation and moral improvement. In this respect, Jean-Marie Piemme is quite right to note that, in the seventeenth century, "the most advanced mode of criticism of the theater is perhaps, in some respects, that which seeks to destroy it."[4] Having less to lose than their opponents in plumbing the murky depths of audience psychology, anti-theatricalists are rather more willing to tackle the full moral and cognitive complexities of spectatorship.

Indeed, identificatory processes form something of a refrain within anti-theatricalist thought. According to Nicole, for example, witnessing a dangerous passion onstage can produce in us "a similar movement, which transforms us in some way, and makes us enter the passion that is being represented."[5] Rather more concisely,

3. Pierre Corneille, *Œuvres complètes*, ed. Georges Couton, 3 vols (Paris: Pléiade, 1980–87), III. 143.

4. Jean-Marie Piemme, "Le théâtre en face de la critique religieuse: un exemple, Pierre Nicole," *XVIIe siècle* 88 (July-September 1970): 49.

5. Pierre Nicole, *Traité de la comédie*, in *Traité de la comédie, et autres pièces d'un procès du théâtre*, ed. Laurent Thirouin (Paris: Champion, 1998), 32–111, 62–64.

Bossuet claims that each spectator "becomes a secret actor,"[6] while Yves de Paris insists that every theatergoer becomes "both spectator and character."[7] One of the period's richest engagements with the question comes from the Oratorian theologian Bernard Lamy, who vividly describes the power of plays, novels, and epics to so draw in their audiences that they seem to embrace a completely new identity. Lamy's account of reading epic in his *Nouvelles réflexions sur l'art poétique* (1668) is perhaps exemplary in this respect:

> Sometimes [the reader] feels his heart full of warlike fire, and he imagines himself fighting; sometimes, stirred by gentler movements, he becomes involved in the intrigues of the work's hero: he is a soldier and a lover like him; and, in a word, he is in his imagination what this hero is, and what he himself would like to be.[8]

Bold and intriguing as such formulations are, we should be wary of leaping to Thirouin's conclusion that the spectator's relationship to the fictional hero is one of "full identification"—not least because the term "identification" does not necessarily have a single, determinate or "full" sense, but rather can cover a range of quite diverse cognitive and aesthetic processes.

This article traces some of these different theories of identification in anti-theatrical thought through the specific optic of dramatic pleasure. Of course, the relationship between identification and pleasure has never been a clear-cut, obvious, or stable one and, despite the period's renewed emphasis on both, there was little theoretical consensus about the nature of either. Both were hotly debated, not only between pro- and anti-theatrical camps but also within these factions themselves. Indeed, we can sometimes see conflicting models of both identification and pleasure at work even within a single theoretical text. As this article will demonstrate, the complex interrelations between identification and pleasure underlie Lamy's theory on various levels, from his most basic precepts of psychology to his specific comments on tragic theater. First, I explore the roles that

6. Jacques-Bénigne Bossuet, *Maximes et réflexions sur la comédie*, in *L'église et le théâtre*, ed. C. Urbain and E. Levesque (Paris: Grasset, 1930), 178–79.

7. Yves de Paris, *Les vaines excuses du pécheur en ses passions*, 2 vols (Paris: Thierry, 1662–64), II. 315.

8. Bernard Lamy, *Nouvelles réflexions sur la poétique*, ed. Tony Ghaereert (Paris: Champion, 1997), 182 (henceforth referenced by page numbers in the text).

pleasure and identification play in Lamy's general model of human psychology. Then my essay moves on to the pleasurably narcissistic relationship that Lamy perceives between poetry (both dramatic and epic) and its audience's passions. Building on and refining Lamy's more general observations, I finally turn to the theater in particular, tracing first the forms of pleasure that identifications with idealized dramatic heroes can produce and finally the curious modes of disidentification and emotional disengagement that specifically tragic pleasure can provoke.[9]

Lamy's *Nouvelles réflexions* form a curious, composite text. Rather than simply condemning the theater from an external perspective, Lamy ostensibly writes from within the conventional realm of poetics and dramatic theory, while using his analysis to condemn all forms of imaginative literature. Lamy's text can thus appear as something of a Trojan Horse, smuggling anti-theatrical arguments into a work that often reads like a more conventional work of poetics. One of Lamy's guiding concerns is the analysis and dissection of aesthetic pleasure, an issue that proves to be as problematic conceptually as it is ethically. Pleasure lies at the very heart of the aesthetic enterprise for Lamy. As he explains in his "Avertissement," although poetry's origins were coarse and rudimentary, "poets gradually applied themselves to composing their works according to the taste of their audiences, whose pleasure was the only rule they followed in constructing their works" (129–30). Aesthetic conventions, in other words, have developed solely in order to maximize the pleasure that poetry can produce in its audiences.

This notion that all literary modes simply cater to public tastes is a familiar refrain among anti-theatricalists, and indeed among some pro-theatrical writers as well. Yet for Lamy this notion reveals a certain identificatory relationship between literary works and their audiences. Poetry, Lamy suggests, offers a reflection of its audience. Although this reflection is not necessarily reliable, since it is refracted through the lens of pleasure, poetry shares a close enough relationship with its audience that the study of the one can, Lamy suggests,

9. Since Lamy tends, throughout the *Réflexions*, to discuss drama and epic alongside each other, using examples from each to illustrate broader points, it would—I believe—be artificial or misleading to focus only on those comments that Lamy makes explicitly or exclusively about drama. On occasion, therefore, I have tacitly applied to the theater claims that Lamy in fact makes about imaginative literature in general.

offer important insights into the other. Crucially, then, poetics is not for Lamy an abstract discipline divorced from the world of human experience. Rather, since the rules of poetry are deeply rooted in human psychology—what he calls "the nature of man" (130)—human nature and the human condition can be analyzed through cultural artifacts such as theater and epic. His own theoretical reflections, he announces, are distinctive precisely because "there are no poetic rules whose principles—that is, the causes of the pleasure produced by poems that obey these rules—they do not uncover" (130). For Lamy, then, poetry puts into practice, and thus alerts the astute reader to, more general principles of human psychology.

Importantly, identification seems to have pride of place among these psychological principles. Far from being limited to the specific relationship between audiences and fictional heroes, identificatory modes seem to underpin even the most general (non-aesthetic) cognitive processes for Lamy. For example, Lamy presents human thought itself as a sort of cognitive embrace in which the soul "is united in some manner with the object of its knowledge" (150). We all have, he argues, a deep-seated desire to engage and "be united" with something external to us. At heart, this aspiration to transcend the self is a holy one, and its ultimate object is union with the divine. A truly Christian soul—one that has achieved this embrace with God—is self-sufficient or, more correctly, finds in God all the satisfaction and inner peace that it seeks: "A soul whose chaste pleasures are all provided by God enjoys a deep peace, and finds enough in this single object of love to still this avidity it has for possessions" (151). For most of us, however, this desire simply reflects our inner discontent, and what Pascal famously calls the "the wretchedness of man without God."[10] In a passage from the *Pensées* that Lamy quotes at length, Pascal explains how the soul craves distraction from the "unbearable pain" of being continually "obliged to live with itself, and to think of itself" (152).[11] Unfortunately for religious moralists like Lamy and Pascal, this desire for union with something external and our craving for *divertissement* (distraction) can easily be hijacked by worldly things; contemplation of worldly matters tears us away both from ourselves and from God.

10. Blaise Pascal, *Pensées*, ed. Philippe Sellier (Paris: Garnier, 1991), 40.
11. Pascal, 201.

The Pascal passage that Lamy quotes is not directly concerned with the theater, but rather with the soul's desire to become oblivious to its own torments through immersion in something external. For Pascal, the theater is just one of many distractions that earthly existence offers us, and like all such *divertissements* it does not so much produce pleasure positively as distract our attention away from our distress and suffering. Lamy develops Pascal's basic observations, both adapting them to the more specific question of dramatic pleasure—as we shall see shortly—and also giving them at points a more identificatory spin. According to Lamy, for example, once some external object has fixed our attention, we might be led to embrace it as part of, or indistinguishable from, our own self; for example, he speaks evocatively of a miser's love for wealth, meaning that his heart is "entirely in his treasure" (178). Metaphorically at least, the individual can thus invest some part of himself in something earthly and external, rather than letting some part reside in its God-allotted place.

On this general level, then, identification and pleasure are not at odds with each other. Since, without God's grace, pleasure is defined at best as the avoidance of displeasure, we crave distraction from ourselves and union with something external. Revealingly, Lamy often figures this need for distraction in spatial terms. Throughout the *Réflexions* Lamy invokes an implicitly spatial rhetoric in which the individual's heart or soul is drawn out from its allotted place and moves outwards toward something external. He uses this rhetoric, for example, when he develops his earlier claim about our cognitive embrace with external objects; as he puts it, when the soul is occupied with such objects, "it leaves itself, and so cannot tell what is happening there" (150). Yet although—as the miser example suggests—this "centrifugal" process can take a range of different objects, the beguiling fictions of theater and epic are in many ways ideally suited to hijacking these spiritual aspirations.

For Lamy, then, the basic processes of cognition involve a certain centrifugal impulse away from the self and into the outside world. Once we consider the dramatic experience more specifically, however, things become rather more complicated. Having been expertly crafted in order to cater to audience tastes, imaginative fictions respond to a more self-centered, "centripetal" movement, in which audiences crave to see their own concerns, passions, and interests reflected back at them. The irresistible gravitational pull of the audience's *amour-propre* (self-love or self-interest) thus provides a complex counterweight to the concomitant centrifugal impulse to escape the self, and holds out the prospect of quite different modes of both identification and pleasure. As Lamy's contemporary Conti claims, we can derive a certain narcissistic pleasure in witnessing ourselves or elements of ourselves onstage: "We like to see portraits of our passions just as we do portraits of ourselves."[12] Far from being distracted from ourselves in a cognitive embrace of something external, it seems, we now wish to be occupied with depictions of passions that we already recognize and experience in ourselves. Lamy broadly echoes Conti's claim when he implies that we each respond to whatever in the dramatic fiction reflects our own dominant character traits and passions: "Ambitious people find in such works images of their ambition, and vindictive types a depiction of the effects of vengeance" (154).

As Conti states, the theater thus offers us "portraits" of our own passions and obsessions, and these portraits can be a source of pleasure. Yet since individual theatergoers can differ widely in their own personal tastes and temperaments, dramatists have learned to home in on those most prevalent passions in order to maximize overall audience pleasure. Furthermore, since love is the most universal of passions, Lamy explains, "the whole work always centers around some amorous intrigue" (156). The pleasure that love plots can produce in us stems from our already fallen, sinful state: "Any sensual mind will be burning with some shameful flame, and will accordingly take pleasure in reading poets' depictions of such foul affections" (156). To this end Lamy paraphrases a passage of St. Augustine's *Confessions*: "I had, he says, a violent passion for dramatic spectacles, which were full of images of my wretchedness, and of amorous flames that entertained the fire that was devouring me" (156).

As I have already suggested, we thus have two conflicting modes of identification. On the one hand, we have a centrifugal desire to vacate our own place and unite ourselves with something external. On the other hand, dramatists also cater to our more centripetal desire to see external things as reflecting our own selves. The problem is that when these two modes of identification operate alongside each other, they do not so much cancel each other out as create a vicious

12. Conti, *Traité de la comédie et des spectacles*, in Nicole, *Traité de la comédie*, 201.

circle. Conti sums up this paradox quite memorably; as he puts it, although we enjoy contemplating portraits of our passions, "these portraits often become our models, and . . . by depicting the passions of others, the theater stirs our soul in such a manner as to awaken our own."[13] In this circular situation, we are trapped in a strange narcissistic relationship, experiencing passions modeled on passions that have themselves been constructed to reflect our own pre-existing tastes. In this respect Conti's use of the word "model" is striking; a passion depicted onstage is indeed both a model (replica) of our own pre-existing passions and a model (exemplum) around which we can shape our own future passions.

If the theater simply reflected our passions back at us passively, there would perhaps be no problem. But as Lamy and his fellow anti-theatricalists recognized, this loop actually fosters and foments our own passions. Crucial to this process is pleasure, something that spectators can experience only by lending their approval to the sinful actions and passions seen onstage. Theater spectators, Lamy insists, "cannot take pleasure in it without esteeming and approving what they see" (166). Pleasure casts a veneer of moral approval over everything witnessed. It can lead us into a mimetic replication of the passions depicted onstage during the performance, and even tempt us into committing similar actions to what we have witnessed after the play: "We are always pleased to imitate whatever we have enjoyed seeing represented" (183).

As Cecila Gallotti points out, many anti-theatricalists evoke this general process through a rhetoric of contagion.[14] Bossuet, for example, condemns "the contagious expression of our illnesses,"[15] while Nicole explains that some passions are "contagious."[16] Lamy, however, tends to favor an imagery of fire rather than contagion. In Augustine's formulation above, the amorous flames onstage "entertain" the fire that devours the spectator. For Lamy too, "a skilled poet gives such fire to those whose movements he depicts that it becomes impossible, while pleasure binds us to them, for us not to be burned by the same flames" (199). Like contagion, fire can spread across the boundary that supposedly separates stage from auditorium. Yet whereas the

13. Conti, 201.

14. Cecilia Gallotti, "Le voile d'honnêteté et la contagion des passions," *Terrain* 22, "Les émotions" (March 1994): 51–68.

15. Bossuet, 136.

16. Nicole, 62.

contagion metaphor implicitly casts spectators as passive, innocent victims of the infectious passions depicted onstage, Lamy's fire imagery reminds us that we are already burning with illicit passions even before we enter the theater. We do not just passively enjoy depictions of desire when we encounter them onstage; rather, we actively seek them out. Perhaps paradoxically, we feel the desire for desire: as Lamy puts it, spectators "want poets to stoke the fire of their passions, which are like the wounds of their souls" (156).

One of the reasons why theater not only reflects spectators' passions but also fosters them is that plays are not the static, pictorial modes of "portraits," "images," and "depictions" that the rhetoric we have so far seen might suggest. The passions we witness onstage are not abstract, atemporal phenomena; they are always embodied within specific fictional characters whose desires, like those of the spectators, can be awoken, thwarted, stifled, or fulfilled as events develop. Indeed, for Lamy at least, the relationship between our enjoyment at contemplating portraits of our passions and portraits of ourselves is not just the analogical one that Conti suggests; if anything, Lamy seems to say that by recognizing that the dramatic hero shares our passions we can come to (mis)recognize him as a reflection of ourselves.[17]

Yet while our self-recognition in the passions depicted onstage is crucial to the general pleasures the theater offers us, our relationship to the dramatic hero is dominated, for Lamy, by a quite different mode of identification. What attracts us to the dramatic hero and focuses our attention on him, Lamy suggests, is less our recognition of some overlap of personality or passions between us and him (although we may well experience this too), but rather his overall presentation as a positive figure. In short, the dramatic hero has to be likeable, and it is this likeability that leads us to identify or empathize with him. Lamy derives this basic premise from a general reflection on human sociability:

> All men have a natural loving inclination toward each other; accordingly, they tend to love those in whom they find certain amiable qualities and with whom they have a sort of sympathy. Men wish for nothing more than to find some person in whom they can place their affections . . . (179)

17. Since Lamy has precious little to say about women spectators or characters, I am following his practice in adopting the universal masculine form here.

Since the most effective of all these "amiable qualities," Lamy suggests, is virtue, poets and playwrights invariably model their heroes on "the idea that those whom they wish to please have of virtue" (165). Yet our affective bond to the attractive hero is not simply one of impersonal, disinterested goodwill; it, too, contains a certain identificatory element. Our natural instinct to invest our affection in anyone who exhibits the requisite "amiable qualities" is reflected, Lamy explains, in a sort of identificatory "sympathy" between us and them— and this sympathy, we shall see, allows us to share in and replicate their own passions.

Before exploring this process in more detail, however, it is worthwhile briefly to consider another mode of identification between us and the dramatic hero. Although our goodwill for the hero's inherent virtue aligns us with him as the focus of narrative interest, we continue to recognize ourselves in his passions and flaws too. What makes this self-recognition particularly pleasurable, claims Lamy, is the fact that the hero is presented as an idealized model of virtue. For Lamy, poets might not technically praise vices, but by presenting flawed heroes positively "they not only make us unashamed to resemble them, but even make us glory in sharing their flaws" (223). In other words, the idealized dramatic character effectively profits from what modern psychologists call the "halo effect": his positive overall presentation, and our desire to regard him as an internally coherent being, lead us to overlook any less reputable elements in his nature, or even to reassess them positively. The hero presents us with an attractive "ideal ego" that not only reflects our passions back at us, but also recontextualizes them in such a way that we now deem them as something positive. In this respect, the dramatic hero offers spectators, "so to speak, the apology for their passions" (165).[18] Accordingly, we bask in his reflected glory even if we share only his negative qualities. Yet perversely, we not only fall victim to the halo effect ourselves, but we also attempt to take advantage of the same effect in other people; as Lamy explains, we readily assume that "those

---

18. Although the situation is of course somewhat reversed with the baser characters of comedy, the spectator nonetheless follows a comparably self-serving logic. Flawed comic characters produce pleasure, Lamy claims, "either because we are pleased, in our disorder, to have companions with whom we share the shame of sin, or because we feel a secret satisfaction in being exempt from the flaws of others" (219). In other words, we either pride ourselves on our superiority to those onstage or seek safety in numbers and are relieved to see others as sinful as ourselves.

who notice these same flaws in us as in these great men will judge that we are similar to them in all other respects" (223). So even here Lamy suggests a certain self-reflexivity in our engagement with the hero: however close our identification with him, we retain throughout a certain awareness of ourselves and the impression we make on others. Indeed, as we shall see below, our dangerous capacity to identify with others is counterbalanced at key points in Lamy's theory by an equally dangerous tendency to disengage ourselves and to see ourselves from a third-person viewpoint.

One of the key consequences of our emotional attachment to the dramatic hero is that we are led to share in his experiences and passions. This is partly, as I suggested earlier, a consequence of what Lamy calls "sympathy"—a natural, instinctual bond between people that allows affective states to be passed from one person to another. As Lamy explains, "as nature has made us for each other, it has bonded us through this sympathy or reciprocal communication of our passions" (224). As this gloss suggests, our "affection" or "love" for others can thus make us receptive to whatever passions or emotions they experience. As he explains, the theater establishes "tight sympathetic bonds" between us and the heroes, so that "we enter all their sentiments more easily, and we embrace all their passions" (198–99). Writers harness our natural inclination toward those we like, producing in us "a strong passion for these heroes" (180) and setting off a process that involves both intellectual and emotional impulses:

> We then wish to know their adventures; we become involved in whatever concerns them, and we find ourselves so tightly bonded to them that we embrace all their passions. We love what they love; we hate what they hate; we are pleased or afflicted along with them. (180)

The hero—who, for Lamy, is always presented as an idealized character—becomes a channel though which the spectator experiences a range of vicarious emotions, some positive, others negative. Furthermore, once it is established, our attachment to the hero appears to be remarkably resilient; not only do we recognize and even welcome the hero's vices, but we are also quite happy to maintain our identification even when the experiences he undergoes and evokes become a source of displeasure for us. Indeed, here and elsewhere Lamy explicitly lists suffering among the range of emotions that we can be led to share with the hero. Our identification thus outlasts the immediate sensation of pleasure that comes from imagining our-

selves as one with the strong and virtuous figure whose adventures
we follow. How pleasurable, though, is it to share a hero's unpleasant
experiences?

Lamy does not give a single coherent answer to this question. He
sometimes implies that we continue to experience pleasure whatever
the hero himself undergoes. He claims, for example, that once we have
become appropriately engaged with the hero our heart "takes pleasure
in being moved by all the various passions produced by the different
states through which the poet leads the hero" (180). Elsewhere, however, the hero's suffering produces more complex responses in Lamy's
spectator. Lamy sometimes suggests that our identification does not
allow us to enjoy sharing the hero's negative emotions indefinitely.
Rather, he insists, dramatists who bring spectators to feel "esteem"
and "love" for the heroes are effectively compelled to reward them, in
order to produce in us the vicarious pleasure that we feel when those
we love are successful (204).

Yet although Lamy's reflections here can certainly help explain
the overall appeal of comedy and epic, he—like his contemporaries—
experiences considerable difficulty in explaining the pleasures specific
to tragedy. Sometimes he suggests that the very intensity of tragic
emotions can produce pleasure by distracting the spectator from his
own *ennui*: "Tragic accidents can strike his mind more forcefully and
so draw him out of himself, where he finds only subjects of sadness
and pain" (219). Elsewhere, though, the thorny theoretical question
of tragic pleasure compels Lamy to revise or nuance his otherwise
categorical insistence on our mimetic replication of the hero's emotions, and to introduce a crucially new element of dis-identification
or emotional disengagement. Despite the narcissistic pleasures that
the theater offers us, we do seem able to retain a certain emotional
distance from the hero that allows us to derive pleasure from experiences that he himself would find dangerous or unpleasant. As Lamy
puts it, "the emotions that we experience on witnessing some misfor-
tune that cannot harm us, produce satisfaction" (181). We do not fully
experience the hero's suffering because the theater produces a certain
aesthetic distance—or perhaps rather an *an*aesthetic distance—in us.
Accordingly, tragedy makes us pleasurably complicit in the hero's
suffering without any of the risks:

The pain we suffer on seeing the misfortunes of someone we judge
worthy of a better fortune is linked, through a marvelous union,

> to contrary sentiments of joy and sweetness. We enjoy weeping for
> sorrows that we do not suffer . . . It is not that others' pain causes us
> satisfaction, but we are glad to see ourselves spared it. (181)

As Lamy's vocabulary here suggests, our response is unexpected and
contradictory, embodying as it does a "marvelous union" of conflicting emotions. Lamy's reasoning here relies on a crucial distinction
between the onstage character and the spectator. Far from being fully
identified with the hero, as Lamy elsewhere suggests, the spectator
of tragedy experiences a certain thrill—of relief or even of *Schaden-
freude*—on being spared the hero's predicament and by remaining
emotionally distinct from him. At the very heart of our identification, it seems, we remain somehow secure in our own experience.

Our pleasure, however, does not consist only in our relief at witnessing misfortunes that we are spared. We also take pleasure, it
seems, in our own capacity for compassion. Far from awakening some
true intersubjective engagement between us and the hero, Lamy suggests, our compassion can actually have quite the opposite effect.
Instead, we risk becoming complicit with the suffering depicted onstage, since we end up deriving pleasure from our own feelings of
compassion, which become for us an end in themselves:

> We imagine that there is nobility in lamenting the misfortunes of
> someone illustrious and persecuted, and hating his enemies . . . We
> feel a certain satisfaction in the fact that we love virtue, and that our
> heart is not unfeeling. (180)

Despite Lamy's earlier claim that witnessing others' suffering does
not directly produce "satisfaction," he acknowledges here that satisfaction does play a role in the pleasures of self-congratulation. Rather
than being a source of true empathy or fellow-feeling, compassion
turns us back upon ourselves in an experience of pure self-indulgence.
We become aware of ourselves, almost as if from an outside perspective, and revel in our own private display of charity and generosity.

As Lamy here implies, whatever pleasure we derive from tragedy
or from onstage misfortunes is essentially indirect. Rather than passively embracing the character's emotions, we take on a third-person
stance toward our own selves and applaud ourselves on our sensitivity and compassion. Our pleasurable distance from the hero is one of
the reasons why plays cannot have the morally improving effect that
others claim. Defenders of the theater, such as Corneille, would insist
that we can never feel fully protected from tragic suffering, precisely

because our supposed resemblance to the hero means that we risk an equivalent fate. Lamy implies here that, at least at the play's tragic conclusion, we are simply too disengaged from the hero to truly learn from his experiences. In the most general terms, then, Lamy agrees with pro-theatricalists that spectators of tragedy move from a general identification with the tragic hero to a moment of dis-identification or disengagement. The crucial point, though, is the moral status of this disengagement. For pro-theatricalists, at the end of the play the spectator disengages from the hero and the flaws that have led to his suffering in a salutary, cathartic move that leaves the spectator morally improved. For Lamy, in contrast, the spectator's disengagement from the hero marks an affective retreat from the negative and unpleasant emotions the hero is experiencing.

Our exploration of identification in Lamy's thought has thus led us in quite an unexpected direction, toward its very opposite. The same writer who offers one of the period's most vivid theoretical accounts of identification, and who understands thought itself as involving a cognitive "union" of soul and object, also acknowledges—sometimes on the same page—strongly anti-identificatory impulses. Far from being plunged into experiences of a tragic hero, or passively contaminated with his emotions, we are at crucial points made forcibly (and pleasurably) aware of our own ontological difference from him, and even start to perceive ourselves from an external third-person perspective. If the soul is malleable enough to merge with other things or people, it is also able to split itself in two and to let one part observe the other. As Lamy implies, what is perhaps more dangerous than our passive, immediate, emotional identification with dramatic fictions is precisely our intellectual capacity to disengage ourselves from these fictions at those very points when some form of empathy might be appropriate or improving. Self-interestedly, we experience our own emotions at one remove, as pleasurable signs of our own moral superiority, and indeed positively welcome fictions that might favorably skew others' judgments of us. To this extent we become performers of our own—not just imaginary "secret actors" during the performance as Bossuet claimed, but rather deceptive and self-deceptive agents on the social stage, craving the illusory pleasures of being identified with heroes in other people's minds rather than truly seeking to emulate their virtues.

EMILIA WILTON-GODBERFFORDE

Unmasking Falsehood: The Theatrical Pattern of Revelation in Nicole and Lamy

In emphasizing the persuasive yet nefarious effect of the theater, anti-theatricalist religious moralists such as Pierre Nicole and Bernard Lamy can also be seen to reinforce, unwittingly, the theater's sway on the spectator. By reminding the reader of the pleasurable and hypnotic experience that a spectacle can generate, they bring to the fore the very elements they are trying to suppress. As Laurent Thirouin rightly notes, "the enemies of the theater are those who believe the most in its power; they take the genre extremely seriously and underline its power and its effectiveness."[1] That said, this feature has so far received insufficient attention. Barbara Vinken mistakenly suggests that Nicole, as a defensive move, abandons the figural schemes of rhetoric altogether, and she fails to appreciate the way in which his writing betrays a susceptibility to the aesthetic experience.[2] Tony Gheeraert does underline the contradictory effect that emerges in Lamy's writing—"in attempting to limit the rise of literature, in assigning a place where it can remain under the control of reason, the Oratorian, despite himself, demonstrates its formidable power"—but he does not go on to analyze this. This article takes this intriguing contradiction as its starting point.[3]

Of course, the anti-theatricalists' purpose in drawing attention to the spectator's reactions is to steer the reader away from such activity

---

1. Laurent Thirouin, *L'aveuglement salutaire: Le réquisitoire contre le théâtre dans la France classique* (Paris: Champion, 1997), 20. Translations throughout are my own.
2. Barbara Vinken, "The Concept of Passion and the Dangers of the Theatre," *Romanic Review* 1 (1992): 55.
3. Bernard Lamy, *Nouvelles réflexions sur l'art poétique*, ed. Tony Gheeraert (Paris: Honoré Champion, 1998), 123.

YFS 130, *Guilty Pleasures: Theater, Piety, and Immorality in Seventeenth-Century France,* ed. Harris and Prest, © 2016 by Yale University.

and put an end to these supposedly ungodly pursuits. Yet in tracing out and firmly rejecting the theatrical enterprise and its effects on the viewer in their metadiscourse, anti-theatrical writers require the reader to dwell specifically on these responses and to reflect upon the process of the theatrical experience. However, it is not simply the focus on the theatrical experience that lets the reader imagine a spectacle being performed before his eyes. The manner in which the writers present their arguments transports the reader into an imagined theatrical space where he is witness to a story enacted before him. The writers achieve this, largely, by reproducing a pattern akin to the theatrical moment of unveiling, a process of revelation and resolution on which I focus in the course of this article.[4] Of course, we should not conflate too uncritically these theoretical arguments with dramatic performance, since they lack the specular dimension and other paralinguistic elements of true theater. Nonetheless, I aim to tease out some of the ways in which Bernard Lamy in the *Nouvelles réflexions sur l'art poétique* (1678)[5] and Pierre Nicole in the *Traité de la comédie* (1667)[6] engage rhetorically with the subject of the theater and, in so doing, underline, echo, and subvert the emotive and aesthetic dimensions they suggest are foregrounded in the viewer's experience of a play.

One of the distinct pleasures associated with the theatrical experience, particularly in the comedic genre, comes from watching the story-telling mechanism unfold: seeing mistakes, falsehoods, misunderstandings, and the consequences such distortions can provoke, then following the process of unveiling and recognition by characters in the play, which eventually leads to some kind of resolution and a restoration of order. This reassuring pattern of complication, resolution, and a neutralizing exposure of what was troubling and deceptive can also be witnessed in the organizational logic of Lamy's and Nicole's texts. In guiding the reader away from what they see as a distorted and dangerous realm and toward the reassuring world of God's truth, they employ a means of disentanglement and re-evaluation

---

4. For a detailed exploration of the process of unveiling within drama, see Terence Cave, *Recognitions. A Study of Poetics* (Oxford: Clarendon Press, 1988), who scrutinizes the patterns set by the Aristotelian requirements of *harmatia*, *peripeteia*, *anagnorisis*, and *catharsis*.

5. Bernard Lamy, *Nouvelles réflexions sur l'art poétique*, ed. Tony Gheeraert (Paris: Honoré Champion, 1998).

6. Pierre Nicole, *Traité de la comédie et autres pièces d'un procès du théâtre*, ed. Laurent Thirouin (Paris: Honoré Champion, 1998). I am using the 1667 version.

that deserves closer scrutiny. On a fundamental level, all rhetoric is inherently theatrical, just as all theater is rhetorical, since both are constructed in order to elicit powerful responses from their audience.[7]

APPROACHES

In presenting the seductive and immoral characteristics of the "poetic art," both Nicole and Lamy map out their approach in clear terms. Nicole states a desire to examine the very mechanics of the performance, rather than simply presenting an abstract commentary that leaves the actual process a mystery: "But the manner to defend oneself from this illusion is, on the contrary, to consider theater not as fanciful speculation, but as an ordinary and common practice that we witness."[8] He sets out the focus of his investigation very methodically:

> [W]e must examine what kind of life actors and actresses lead; what the subject matter and aim of the plays is; and what effects they normally produce in the minds of those who perform them, or who watch them be performed; what impressions they leave on them; and we must then examine if all this has some bearing on the life, feelings and duties of a true Christian.[9]

Just as a dramatist constructs his fiction, Nicole constructs his argument carefully in order to provoke the right response in his reader.[10] Yet unlike a playwright, who contemplates the design of the play in order to create a work that will entertain, the anti-theatricalist is interested in examining the process and the constituent parts of the theatrical enterprise, in order to better understand the craft and subsequently expose its artifice to the viewer.

Like Nicole, Lamy is also interested in the mechanics and structural form of plays. He seeks to analyze the building blocks of a play, looking at "the premise, the complications and the denouement,"[11]

---

7. Indeed, in this text Lamy condemns all imaginative literature, and in often deliberately analyzing epic and drama alongside one another, he emphasizes the dramatic features inherent in both these kinds of constructed fictions.

8. Nicole, 34.

9. Ibid.

10. See Louis Marin, "La critique de la représentation théâtrale à l'âge classique," *Continuum. Problems in French Literature from the Late Renaissance to the Early Enlightenment* 2 (1990): 81–105.

11. Lamy, 203.

and throughout the second part of the text, he examines particularly closely the rules governing the "poetic art," including genre distinctions and how different devices are employed to generate a specific effect. He presents a precise breakdown of how the story-telling mechanism unfolds. He identifies how, for curiosity to be aroused, the presentation needs to be both clear and obscure. While what we understand of the plot needs to be clear to us, a certain opacity means we are still left with things undisclosed and want to discover more.[12] The plot's complication comes when an unexpected difficulty emerges suddenly, "which places a powerful obstacle that prevents the hero from achieving his goals."[13] The "difficulties" and "delays" that block the resolution of the main action that we want to see conclude are, as he puts it, "the salt that awakens curiosity."[14] With disdain, Lamy suggests that poets manipulate us by making us pay for the information they gradually disclose. In this respect, he differentiates his own discourse from such a calculated craft that, he suggests, toys with expectation before finally presenting a denouement through a peripeteia or anagnorisis (moment of recognition). Lamy's text is not so formulaically mapped out as these fictional models. Despite his refusal to reveal information progressively, the *Nouvelles réflexions* do, on closer inspection, present a discernible line of progress and unveiling.

In the first section, Lamy presents individuals as moving from primitive, misguided beings to curious seekers of truth. He then traces the activities that perpetuate this blindness and keep us distracted. Further obstacles that keep us separated from God are also discussed, and the danger of love, which is at the heart of the poetic enterprise, is explored. Focusing on truth in the last three chapters, Lamy presents the way in which truth is thwarted, ending by suggesting that a distinct path is forged toward "criminal things" that depart further and further "from the end which we ought to reach."[15]

We see therefore that the overall narrative that unfolds is one of viewing falsehood perpetuated, scrutinized, and unveiled. Yet, importantly, Lamy does not conclude with some kind of resolution or positive restoration of order. His message suggests that, as long as we are exposed to poetry, we continue to be trapped in futile ideas

12. Ibid., 204.
13. Ibid.
14. Ibid., 140.
15. Ibid., 163.

and deceived by illusions.[16] This paralyzed position is a striking way to end the process he has sketched out. Indeed he makes this position particularly memorable by reaffirming and echoing this entrapment and paralysis at the end of the second part of his text. Here, the stagnant position of being immersed in deception is presented by likening the person who is caught up in a fictional world and imagines himself to be a hero, to the character of Don Quixote. By ending with this deluded fictional hero, Lamy reinforces the idea that not only is the reader of fiction trapped in his fanciful deception but also that our point of comparison can only be a fictional figure, so tightly entrenched have we become in this fabricated world. Instead of presenting a lucid position of distance from the theater at the end, Lamy shows the illuminating process of disentangling earlier on, throughout his analysis. The ending, rather, envelops the reader in the obfuscation that Lamy's argument worked to dispel, thus providing a cautionary reminder of the risk of remaining enclosed in this fallacious thinking.

Nicole's ending is markedly different. He arrives at his conclusion through a logical charting of those elements within the theater that permanently threaten us; he describes our need to be entertained and hence the way we are easily entranced by the theater. He also scrutinizes its different features, systematically contrasting the values of Christianity with those found in the theater (all familiar territory, also examined by Lamy). However, his ending is much bolder and more climactic. The penultimate chapter stresses the insubstantial nature of all things of this world and leads to the final chapter, "What must be the object of horror and aversion for the Christian" (number 35). This section underlines the irrevocable nature of sin but the saving power of grace:

> Sin has opened men's eyes to help them enjoy the vanities of the world, but grace, through Christianity, in opening the soul's eyes to the things of God, keeps them shut in relation to secular things. This blinding is much more beneficial than the wretched sight that sin provides.[17]

This spiritual blinding is presented as a definitive answer to the problems explored throughout the text. It is a striking ending, paradoxi-

---

16. Ibid., 168.
17. Nicole, 108.

cally grounding enlightenment in blindness; by blacking out the vain temptations through grace, Nicole grounds the process of revelation in spiritual terms. However, reading against the text, we can see a parallel in how he works toward a dramatic climax and a conclusion where all is stripped bare.

EMPHASIZING THE DANGERS OF THE THEATER

For both Nicole and Lamy, the theater is a corrupting force, and both describe it as a school for vice.[18] For Nicole, theater "by its very nature is a school and a training in vice, since it is an art where one has to stir up vicious passions within oneself."[19] Similarly, Lamy writes that "Experience has always shown that the theater is a very poor school for virtue; and that the techniques poets employ to correct men's vices are better suited to fostering their vice than delivering them from it."[20] Both writers, in line with the standard criticism of Christian moralists of the seventeenth century, see all "poetry"[21] as a dangerous chimerical construct that transports its audience away from God. They rehearse standard contemporary arguments against all fiction, and specifically against the theater,[22] based on ancient suspicions concerning mimesis and on theological discussions of unholy activities. In particular, they stress that the theater has a captivating power over our emotions and leads us to indulge in dangerous passions.[23] By focusing on an alternative creation that is not of God's making, they argue, we turn away from what should be the real focus of our attention. By enjoying the theater we waste valuable time that should be spent on nobler pursuits; and, as we identify with the characters of the fictive realm, our critical and moral senses become blurred.[24] The aim of both the *Traité de la comédie* and the *Nouvelles réflexions sur l'art poétique* is to draw attention to these modes of

18. See particularly Henry Phillips, *The Theatre and its Critics* (Oxford: Oxford University Press, 1980) and Thirouin, *L'aveuglement salutaire*.

19. Nicole, 38.

20. Lamy, 221.

21. Lamy says he intends to examine the rules of epic poetry and dramatic poetry although he is aware of drama's unique status as a visual art.

22. See Phillips, *Theatre and its Critics*, 87–113.

23. On how Lamy specifically views identificatory processes and the audience's experience of pleasure, see Joseph Harris's article in the present volume.

24. For a thorough analysis of the way anti-theatricalists (and those in support of the theater) describe the imagined spectator's response to the effects of a performance and how they construct the spectator, see Joseph Harris, *Inventing the Spectator:*

entrapment, so as to unmask them and help the reader turn away from such beguiling charms.

We can appreciate the irony that in trying to distance themselves from the object of their contempt, Nicole and Lamy employ the devices of the same art that they condemn. With such devices, they also end up leading the reader to fixate on the very subject matter that they deem so perilous. Nicole shows an awareness of this overlap and how he risks exposing his reader to such "dangerous" subject matter by focusing on this material. To discuss how even the most horrible passions can be presented in such a way as to become appealing to the spectator, he examines Corneille's *Horace*.[25] Providing a sizeable extract of the speech under scrutiny, Nicole argues that Camille's angry tirade to her brother (in act 4, scene 5), if stripped of all the beauty and gloss of the language furnished by the poet, would be nothing more than the detestable outburst of a crazed girl whose insane passion violates all the laws of nature. Importantly, Nicole then states that he has presented such examples because "they are less dangerous to recount," in terms of subject matter, and suggests that there are far more extreme examples that he deliberately eschews: "It is true that poets use this artifice to disguise vices in matters much more pernicious than the latter."[26] By insisting on his careful selection of citations, Nicole seems to suggest that he can protect the reader from the more perilous influence of the art. However, in dealing with that very subject matter and evoking it for the reader, inevitably, he cannot avoid this close encounter with the material he finds so disturbing (albeit as a text, not as a performance); nor can he avoid exposing it to his reader (even if in a second-hand, mediated fashion).

Both writers show an awareness of the playwright constructing a piece for an audience, and then reflect upon how the putative audience is invited to respond. How, though, do they present their corrective responses to the deviant "instruction" imparted through theater? Both Nicole and Lamy present didactic arguments that propose to unveil and expose what threatens theater spectators. In aiming to deliver their message in an unflinching and direct manner, and in

Subjectivity and the Theatrical Experience in Early Modern France (Oxford: Oxford University Press, 2014).
  25. Corneille, *Horace*, 4.4.1195–1202.
  26. Nicole, 78.

making their aims and their criticism of the theater so explicit, both Nicole and Lamy can contrast their writing with what they see to be the more ambiguous and insidious process of the arousal and the disturbance of the passions that playwrights produce. They constantly criticize the murky and slow-working effects that the passions within the theater can have on the viewer or reader. For Nicole, we are worked upon through a slow process of repetition and attrition; "the spirit is gradually tamed,"[27] and even if an author may limit his character through what he chooses to write about that character, he has very limited control over the cascade of emotions his writing will subsequently evoke in reader or viewer: "The author stops it within his characters by the stroke of his pen: but he does not stop it in the same way in those in whom he has elicited the emotion."[28] Similarly, although more prosaically, Lamy responds to those who argue that works of art have no effect on them by stating that it is merely a question of time: "The works of poets distract the spirit not only when one reads them, but even after one has finished with them."[29]

Yet even in trying to distance themselves from this unpredictable, threatening force that lingers and works on the mind of the reader, Lamy and Nicole hope that their emphatic denunciations will have a lasting impact. Indeed, Nicole presents this constant assault on the reader/spectator in a vivid fashion. In chapter 8, he describes how the devil knows how to lie in wait and take his time until the feelings he had implanted beforehand start to take hold. The pull between good and evil is presented as a cosmic drama where different forces attempt to conquer the human heart. Life, through the "word of life" wrestles with death through the "word of the devil."[30] Both can remain lodged in the human heart for a long time without producing any emotional effect.

The righteous God, the devil in his stealth, and humans in all their vulnerability, provide a compelling cast of characters in the account of the psychic struggle that occurs when susceptible audiences are exposed to plays and novels. The process is described with dramatic momentum, since the frightful onslaught happens in different stages:

27. Ibid., 38.
28. Ibid., 44.
29. Lamy, 149.
30. Nicole, 48.

[T]he devil himself is sometimes satisfied with filling the memory with these images, without going any further, and without creating any other perceptible temptation; and then, after a long time, he stirs them up and awakens them without our even remembering how they came to us in the first place, in order to bring the fruits of death to them.[31]

The reader is constantly reminded of the slippery nature of exposure to dangerous material and these stark reminders punctuate the texts with anticipation and foreboding. Nicole also shows an ability to portray the process of ensnarement with a sense of suspenseful unease:

[T]he descents of the soul are long, they make advances and involve prior designs, and it often happens that we succumb to temptations only because we have been weakened at moments that seemed of no importance, it being certain that he who scorns the little things commits to falling little by little.[32]

This gradual process of descent, in its barely perceptible yet incremental onslaught, is exposed, and its pace and oppressive momentum replicated in the critical texts. The process is somewhat different from a sudden downfall onstage, however, since both writers present the soul's descent from a more reassuring position of security, with the slippage exposed from the start. The stealth and subsequent fall described is, nonetheless, threatening specifically because the victim is caught out and not conscious of his gradual entrapment.

UNMASKING THE POWER OF POETRY

In order to expose the true horrors of the theater, the dramatist's technical artistry must be picked apart. Interestingly, in attempting to unveil elements that should then rightly be obscured, Lamy suggests that poets may work at presenting complications and then elucidations in terms of the plots they construct, but they also include "rare and extraordinary things," merely to mask imperfections and the unsatisfactory and finite nature of what they have to offer.[33] Yet in detailing the very features condemned for concealing such falsehood, Lamy infuses his own text with their appealing nature by providing a compelling list of a diverse assortment of such material. He stirs up

31. Ibid., 50.
32. Ibid., 48.
33. Lamy, 145.

an excitement for the fictive world that encompasses journeys across the earth and into outer space, a variety of geographical terrains and meteorological features, a range of different people and fantastical and monstrous creatures:

> All that encompasses the heavens and the earth becomes subject matter for [poets'] verses; the trajectory of the planets, the movement of the stars, rainstorms, hailstorms, lightning, thunder, mountains, plains, forests, harvests, fountains feature in all their descriptions: they open the bowels of the earth to describe to us what happened there: they speak of the lives of men, of wars of princes, of combats, of sieges of cities; of customs and habits of different people, in an extraordinary and new manner . . . they let their imagination soar based on chimeras, centaurs and other monsters that we never find in nature, to further surprise men through these extraordinary figures.[34]

Similarly, Lamy's description of events depicted in fictional accounts (which he condemns for intoxicating the reader or viewer by means of a barrage of information) conveys a breathless excitement as he lists the range and intensity of bloodshed:

> They know how to stir up the imagination powerfully through rare events, somber deaths, bloody wars, extraordinary stratagems, sieges of cities, combats, states overthrown, or some new empires founded: in a word, all the things which poets recount are capable of arresting the spirit, and of turning it toward them through their innovation, rarity and their grandeur.[35]

This confident and hyperbolic account of these extraordinary and tumultuous happenings can be seen to echo the bombastic rhetoric of the braggart soldier, a popular character of the comedic tradition. Matamore, in Corneille's *L'illusion comique*, famously boasts of his extraordinary skill and mighty feats that, at one point, include a list of all the different buildings and architectural features that his sword could demolish:

> Yes but the sparks that it [the sword] would emit when released from
>   its prison
> Would in an instant burn down the house,
> Then devour slates and gutters,
> Ridges, battens, rafters, jambs, corners, spinnerets,

34. Ibid., 146.
35. Ibid., 148.

Braces, lintels, columns, joists,
Sections of walls, jobs, rails, laths, girders,
Doors, gates, locks, bolts, tile, stone,
Lead, iron, plaster, cement, paint, marble, glass,
Cellars, wells, courtyards, steps, rooms, boudoirs, attics,
Pantries, studies, patios and stairs.[36]

Although I am not suggesting here that Lamy's text is intended to be comic like the speech by the coward who ridiculously vaunts his military prowess, the dizzying array of activities presented is given a fervor and an excessive dimension that reminds us of the awe-inspiring accounts of the stage character, emphasizing the violent energy that "strikes at the imagination" and its preposterous nature.

UNMASKING THE POWER OF SPEECH

Nicole's prose is more restrained than Lamy's, and there are no such instances of the moralist enumerating the effects and being transported by their evocation in the same way that Lamy, despite himself, seems to demonstrate. However, Nicole does show a certain sensitivity to the power of language, noting that plays not only excite the passions but teach their language.[37] His analysis leads us to contemplate the process of hearing and watching the actors in a play. By quoting particular verses that arouse pleasure among the audience, he replays the experience of their pronouncement and reminds the reader of this moment of witnessing speeches and enjoying the sentiments expressed therein. In chapter 17, for example, Nicole criticizes the false opinions contained within Corneille's poetry and how they account for the pleasure one feels. He quotes Rodrigue in *Le Cid*, who boldly asserts that he will not repent of having killed the man who insulted his father and, charting the sequence of cause and effect, declares that he would act in the same way again.[38] Nicole pauses over these words by quoting the character to emphasize what he sees as "the corruption of the mind," but this allows the reader to conjure up the episode he may have seen performed on stage and imagine the character defiantly voicing these words.

36. Pierre Corneille, *L'illusion comique*, in *Œuvres complètes*, ed. Georges Couton (Paris: Gallimard, 1980), 3.4.747–756.
37. Nicole, 58.
38. *Le Cid* (1660), 2.4.871–872, 875–78.

Lamy underlines the specific live nature of performance and the fact that, in drama, the poet does not speak but has characters acting out the action.[39] In voicing their feelings on stage, they communicate them for us, and Lamy underscores how the enunciation and the heightened tone excite ideas within our soul.[40] He does not provide extracts from theatrical works that, as in Nicole's text, summon forth the experience in a particularly direct manner, but nonetheless he does point to the distinct power of the communicative act of speaking. (Lamy states that we are designed to have a shared empathy in feeling with others so that whenever we hear a vicious person, if they speak strongly, we are persuaded to share his viewpoint.)[41] In evoking this "poison" that can infect us, he attempts to make us particularly vigilant in terms of what we allow ourselves to hear, but he also has us muse over the dynamic of speaker and listener and contemplate the natural response of being engaged and persuaded by someone voicing their passion. As I have demonstrated, then, the passion that both Nicole and Lamy seek to circumscribe and reject is nevertheless reawakened in their evocations of the theater.

Overall, for Nicole, the process of unmasking the mechanism of the theatrical enterprise is an attempt to expose the very emptiness upon which it is founded and of which it is composed: "For if all temporal things are nothing but figures and shadows without form, we can say that plays are but shadows of shadows and figures of figures."[42] One expects the process of unveiling to uncover something; for Nicole this "something" is, rather, a nothingness. The play-world may seem to be teeming with action and adventures the complications of which are progressively disentangled, but Nicole reveals these representations to be hollow signifiers with no substantial signified reality. In this way, the theatrical mechanism of unveiling can be seen as distinctly different from Nicole's efforts. Within the fiction of the play-world, there is always information to uncover or some truth to expose, and this drives the play on to its resolution; Nicole, however, suggests that if we investigate the fundamental elements that make up the spectacle, we uncover only "a very

39. Lamy, 208.
40. Ibid., 224.
41. Ibid.
42. Nicole, 108.

particular void and nothingness."[43] And yet, of course, this process of uncovering does still have the means to enlighten since it is in exposing theater's insubstantiality that Nicole can then lead his reader back to contemplating the reality of God's world and to focus on what is worthwhile.

Similarly, as Lamy exposes the essential vanity of the fictive counterpart world, this exposure becomes a productive means to reveal what is preferable to this deceptive distraction. He shows that readers can find justification for their vice in the fictional realm, which is created to distort the truth and flatter them, since "the ambitious find there that we follow ambition without any danger: the vindictive exact their vengeance and go unpunished: the miserly find their riches acquired without difficulties."[44] He also underlines how his investigation of the source of pleasure in poetry leaves no aspect of the discovery process unturned, for "all the principles of the rules of poetry are unveiled here."[45] Furthermore, he views these discoveries as being of considerable importance and interest to a large number of people ("these are very important revelations and which it will please everyone to know"), because what he aims to reveal is no less than the nature of man, an endeavor that involves entering his mind and heart.[46] Although, for Lamy, what the fictional world reveals is merely a predictable repetition of what readers and viewers want to see and feel, he understands his process of discovery as offering something new and providing us with a deeper insight into the nature of our being.

Despite these virtuous and ambitious intentions, a crucial contradiction in aim and effect can be seen in both Lamy's and Nicole's texts because, as I have shown, in attempting to make the reader shun the material under scrutiny, they awaken an interest in its various characteristics and abilities to entrance. Although their overall proclaimed objective is not to concentrate on these particular features but to use them as a means to develop a critical distance, in revealing themselves to be sensitive and attuned to the various appealing devices, their rhetoric unmasks the rhetoric of the texts they shun. The

43. Nicole, 108. The Platonist tradition of the *Republic* still exerted a powerful influence for these writers, as can be seen from such a description. The "nothingness" described is clearly an allusion to Plato's cave.
44. Lamy, 157.
45. Lamy, 130.
46. Ibid.

writers' stress on the power and emotive sway of drama transforms their supposedly descriptive accounts of the theater into powerful performative evocations of the experience of witnessing dramatic performance. The mental space these writers ask the readers to use when contemplating the stage space and their position as a recipient of this fictional display means that those who engage with the texts of both Lamy and Nicole are ultimately invited to be more than mere readers of words on a page.

MICHAEL CALL

Comedic Wars, Serious Moralists: Genre, Gender, and Molière's *L'école des femmes*

The evolution of the *querelle de l'École des femmes* and its eventual spillover into the larger debate about theatrical morality can be summarized concisely by the first few words of the printed title page to Molière's controversial play: *L'école des femmes, comédie.* The phrase contains two nouns—*femmes* (women or wives) and *comédie* (play or comedy)—that function in similar ways in seventeenth-century French as both genus and species, that is, as both general categories and as subsets of those categories. Genre and gender, and more specifically the ways in which Molière's play challenged their traditional strictures, served as major engines for the polemical texts that followed: at first, concerns over the play's redefinition of genre—and of theater's aims in general—contributed significantly to the literary quarrel that erupted shortly after the play's premiere; later, the issue of gender roles, and the play's didactic potential to form them, moved the discussion squarely into the sights of the moralists.

It can be difficult to take the *querelle de l'École des femmes* seriously, particularly in the context of the century's more solemn discussions of theater and morality or the opposition mounted against *Tartuffe* and *Dom Juan.* Robert McBride, however, has argued that *L'école des femmes* represents an important turning point for the period's treatment of theater. In his brief but insightful article, McBride distinguishes three phases to the larger *querelle du théâtre*:

> (a) the internal "querelle" in the theatre about its moral function and the means of achieving it, in which the emphasis is placed upon ways to improve moral tone and content, and this extends roughly from 1630 until 1660; (b) the radical questioning of the theatre's right to exist, extending from the early 1660s until the early 1690s; (c) the final phase in which the *modus vivendi* of the Church and the theatre

YFS 130, *Guilty Pleasures: Theater, Piety, and Immorality in Seventeenth-Century France,* ed. Harris and Prest, © 2016 by Yale University.

virtually disappears, and a hardening of attitudes takes place, lasting until the early years of Louis XV's Regency.[1]

McBride dates the beginning of the second phase to the premiere of *L'école des femmes* and "the subsequent 'Guerre comique' (December 1662-March 1664),"[2] although the connection is not universally accepted. Laurent Thirouin, for example, includes in his detailed chronology of the era's broad anti-theatrical controversy only the event seen traditionally as the end of the dispute set off by Molière's play: Louis XIV's decision in 1664 to stand as godfather to Molière's first son, which was meant to quell any further attacks against the actor/playwright's family life.[3] While Thirouin mentions documents relating to *Dom Juan* and *Tartuffe*, the earlier flurry of plays and other writings provoked by *L'école des femmes* go unexamined, a tacit commentary perhaps on the lack of a clear connection between the two quarrels.

While McBride maintains that the response to Molière's play served as a pivotal bridge between these phases, his article does not elaborate the ways in which the *querelle* changed the terms of the debate from theater's purification to its suppression. I would argue that the *querelle*'s true relevance for theatrical censure and censorship is ironically to be found in its failures: the subject matter and tone of the polemical pieces demonstrate the inability of the literary and theatrical fields to deal internally with the revolutionary changes effected by Molière's new ethics and aesthetics of comedy. The important corollary to this notion is that the more perceptive readers of *L'école des femmes* and the moral questions that it raises are not to be found among either Molière's proponents or opponents during the *querelle* proper—they belong instead to the moralists writing after the narrower theatrical dispute had ended.

This is not to imply that issues of morality, decency, and sexuality were alien to the earlier quarrel. Joan DeJean has emphasized the importance of the play and its aftermath, situating Molière's work within a broader cultural movement that saw the emergence of a new and secularized definition of "bad books," complete with the creation of a governmental book police in 1667 to try to suppress

1. Robert McBride, "The Evolution of the 'Querelle du Théâtre' during the Seventeenth Century in France," *Seventeenth-Century French Studies* 3 (1981): 30.
2. Ibid., 31.
3. Laurent Thirouin, *L'aveuglement salutaire: Le réquisitoire contre le théâtre dans la France classique* (Paris: Champion, 1997), 268.

them.[4] DeJean sees in these events a defining moment for public *obs-cénité* (obscenity), a term that Molière popularized during the quarrel, and pays significant attention to the furor incited by the most inflammatory scene of *L'école des femmes*, the *scène du le*, infamous for its prominent hanging definite article "le." DeJean's depiction of Molière as the modern writer who "launched obscenity" lends support to McBride's reading of the initial *querelle* as a watershed moment for debates about theater's morality, and she is certainly right to draw attention to the significance of this scene for the resulting literary polemic, since none of the major texts fails to mention it.[5]

A closer look at these polemical texts, however, illustrates the extent to which this description needs nuancing. In the first place, Molière's *scène du le* hardly qualifies as the most licentious moment in seventeenth-century theater, even if we limit our investigation to the immediate participants in the *querelle*.[6] Secondly, issues of dramatic decency, while present in the quarrel, do not necessarily occupy pride of place. In fact, perhaps the most surprising aspect of the quarrel for the modern reader is that Molière's critics spend as much time discussing the size of the rock that Agnès throws at Horace as they do condemning the notorious *scène du le*. In other words, many of the criticisms leveled at Molière concern not public decency, but issues of verisimilitude and the rules of the French seventeenth-century stage, as Molière's opponents take great pains to attack issues such as Arnolphe's generosity, the play's setting in the street, the plausibility of Agnès's character, or the superfluous farcical scenes involving the servants or the notary.

Furthermore, when Molière's critics cite the infamous *scène du le*, they often do so as much to capitalize on the prurience and humor that it evokes as to condemn it. In Donneau de Visé's play *Zélinde*

---

4. Joan DeJean, *The Reinvention of Obscenity: Sex, Lies, and Tabloids in Early Modern France* (Chicago: University of Chicago Press, 2002), 122–23.

5. Ibid., 121. DeJean also argues that Molière himself was the primary instigator of the quarrel, writing that the author "provoked controversy in order to obtain the success his still-fledgling company needed" (97). This view has more recently been advocated by Georges Forestier and Claude Bourqui in their article "Comment Molière inventa la querelle de *L'école des femmes* . . . ," *Littératures classiques* 81 (2013): 185–97.

6. Poisson's *Le Baron de la crasse* (1662), for example, leaves no doubt regarding the sexual appetite of the valet Crispin, whose courting is described in the opening scene of the play within a play by Catin (whose name, of course, has bawdy connotations amply developed in the play's prefatory poems).

(1663), the character Argimont brings up the *le* in a scene calculated to mirror Molière's; the repetition of the article becomes comical as the female characters keep insisting that Argimont leave the *the* (*le*) alone.[7] And in *Le portrait du peintre* (1663), Boursault exploits the innuendo even more daringly than Molière had done:

ORIANE. That *the* stayed in my head all night,
    My dear; that *the* charms all the gentlemen.
LE COMTE. Indeed, there are few who don't like it;
    The beauty of that *the* has no equal.
CLITIE. It's true, that *the* pleases a lot of people;
    It's a *the* expressly made for sensitive people.[8]

The decision by the actors of the Hôtel de Bourgogne to sing the bawdy *Chanson de la coquille* at the conclusion of a performance of Boursault's play further illustrates the fact that Molière's opponents were not necessarily seeking to avenge offended propriety.[9] All in all, they seem to have followed the advice given by the titular character of *Zélinde*: "Make people laugh like [Molière] does, and you will succeed; they're only on his side because he entertains them: heap on the satire, align yourself with the taste of the times and you will see if they won't say that you have as much talent as [Molière]."[10]

Such imitation, though, was problematic, as Bélise points out in Robinet's *Panégyrique de l'École des femmes* (1663):

[Molière] has ruined the most beautiful and decent entertainment that we had, and I'm horror-struck by the monsters to which his example has given birth on all our stages. Aren't these fine things, these *Secrétaires de Saint Innocent*, these *Miracles du mépris*, *L'intrigue des carrosses*, *Colin-maillard*, and I don't know how many other shambles [*fatras*], some of which followed *Les précieuses* and *Le cocu imaginaire*, and others of which preceded or accompanied *L'école des*

7. Jean Donneau de Visé, *Zélinde ou la véritable critique de l'École des femmes*, in *La querelle de l'École des femmes*, ed. Georges Mongrédien, vol. 1 (Paris: Société des Textes Français Modernes, 1971), 30. Hereafter referred to as *La querelle* in these notes.

8. Edmé Boursault, *Le portrait du peintre ou La contre-critique de l'École des femmes*, in *La querelle*, vol. 1, 127. With the exception of quotations from Molière, all translations from French are my own.

9. Forestier and Bourqui comment that the *Chanson de la coquille* was "neither more nor less coarse than a number of bawdy songs that abound in the anthologies of the era" (Molière, *Œuvres completes*, ed. Georges Forestier and Claude Bourqui, vol. 2 [Paris: Gallimard, 2010], 1605). Their observation, however, underscores that the Hôtel de Bourgogne was certainly not taking the moral high ground on the issue of obscenity.

10. Boursault, *Zélinde*, in *La querelle*, vol. 1, 62–63.

maris and *L'école des femmes*, to compete with them for the honor of entertaining decent people.[11]

In many respects Robinet is the most perceptive of Molière's adversaries, and Bélise's comment points to the important fact that if Donneau de Visé, Boursault, or Montfleury reproach Molière for chasing refined and serious theater from the stage, they do so through theatrical vehicles that are largely superficial adaptations of Molière's *Critique de l'École des femmes* or *Impromptu de Versailles*. Swelling the ranks of the *fatras* decried by Bélise, these plays show that Molière's "monster" (to use Bélise's term) is quickly becoming a new theatrical standard.

It is in this sense that the title page of *L'école des femmes* acquires new significance. In the eyes of the playwright's opponents, Molière's use of the word *comédie* is not a boilerplate statement of genre, but an aggressive and controversial label that redraws boundaries in ways that menace the mid-century identity of comedy. In addition, just as the French term operates for the era on both specific and general levels, Molière's monstrous comedy represents a threat that could be called synecdochic: the part threatens to subsume the whole, eliminating other theatrical varieties through its burgeoning popularity.

The unease caused by the play's novelty translates into the purported bemusement of the audience or reader in the texts of Molière's opponents. As Robinet writes regarding the ending, "You're not sure if you should laugh or cry."[12] Donneau de Visé notes, "This play produced entirely new results; everyone thought it bad and everyone rushed to attend it. The ladies criticized it and went to see it. It triumphed without pleasing, and it pleased many who didn't think it was good."[13] He adds, "Never have so many good and bad things been seen together."[14] Robinet will mention this bewilderment particularly in connection with the play's most notorious scene, citing "the innuendo of the *the*, which makes members of the fair sex lose their composure, unsure of whether it is more appropriate to laugh or to blush."[15] In each of these cases, Molière's opponents point to a

---

11. Charles Robinet, *Panégyrique de l'École des femmes ou Conversation comique sur les œuvres de M. de Molière*, in *La querelle*, vol. 1, 197.
12. Ibid., 209.
13. In *La querelle*, vol. 1, xiv.
14. Ibid.
15. *Panégyrique de l'École des femmes*, 208.

slippage, a disturbance of the narrow generic constraints of comedy and farce, and they project their own anxieties onto a supposedly perplexed audience, blindsided by a play that they cannot categorize and that produces contradictory results.

But such a critical move shifts the terms of the debate dangerously onto the very grounds that Molière would propose. In *La critique de l'École des femmes* (1663), Molière has his advocates claim that the play does not violate any of the theatrical rules (a dubious argument at best), and, more importantly, promotes a radically simple rule for judging theatrical works able to be applied by any member of the audience or any reader, no matter how cultured or ignorant: the rule of pleasure. After redefining the rules of Horace and Aristotle as simple observations of good sense, Dorante states in scene 6, "I wonder— isn't the greatest rule of all that you must give pleasure to the public? And if a play has done that, hasn't it followed the right path? How can a whole audience be mistaken about such things? Isn't a person the best judge of his own enjoyment?"[16] Dorante continues, "We should let ourselves go, and enjoy the things that give us that gut feeling of satisfaction. We shouldn't keep looking for reasons to spoil our own enjoyment."[17]

But Dorante is not the only or the first of Molière's characters in the *querelle de l'École des femmes* to sweep away rules in favor of simple pleasure. That honor must go to Agnès, whose approach to personal relationships anticipates both the conclusion and the terms of Dorante's method for judging theater. The shared logic between Agnès's ethics and Dorante's aesthetics serves to highlight the other troubling noun on the play's title page that, like *comédie*, can serve as either part or whole: *femmes*. While Molière's earlier adversaries had amply demonstrated their unease at the prospect that Molière's specific *comédie* (comedy) would become synonymous with *comédie* (theater) in general, they were startlingly (or perhaps even willingly) tone-deaf to what undoubtedly should have been the true scandal of the play: the sexual emancipation of Agnès. Arnolphe's central fear is of women who do not act like proper wives, and Agnès's progression in the play from prospective subservient wife to independent desiring (and desirable) woman is not only the realization of Arnolphe's worst

16. Molière, *The School for Wives Criticized*, in *The Misanthrope, Tartuffe, and Other Plays*, tr. Maya Slater (Oxford: Oxford UP, 2001), 96.
17. Ibid.

nightmare, but also that of a phallogocentric society determined to maintain male superiority through the appropriation of reason and regulations, as exemplified in Arnolphe's *Maximes du mariage*. The play's title consequently moves from a possible reference to Arnolphe's failed "school"—his attempt at creating a perfect wife through education—to a meta-theatrical reference in which the play as a whole functions as a school for women, alerting them to the ways in which a patriarchal society tries to force upon them a certain construction of the feminine, or transform them into what Foucault termed "docile bodies."[18]

Agnès successfully resists Arnolphe's attempts at ideological brainwashing through an ethics of pleasure. When Arnolphe mobilizes religious prohibitions, telling her that heaven is upset by Horace's visit, Agnès responds, "Why should heaven be cross? / It's much the most delicious thing I've come across."[19] In the final act, Arnolphe tells Agnès that she should have banished her feelings for Horace, to which Agnès replies, "But how can you control the instincts of your heart?"[20] Arnolphe's stultifying education has left Agnès without the ability to reason with her would-be tyrant in any language other than that of the most spontaneous and natural emotion.

While Molière's opponents in the *querelle de l'École des femmes* objected to Agnès's character on grounds of verisimilitude, they showed a bafflingly misguided (or perhaps disingenuous) understanding of the gender instructions provided in Molière's "school," arguing repeatedly that Molière's play was derogatory toward women and aimed at fostering a stifling patriarchy. The title character of *Zélinde* objects to Arnolphe's line, "A woman who writes knows more than she should," exclaiming: "What! Criticizing women and intelligence both! Undoubtedly he wants us to be as stupid and ignorant as his Agnes."[21] In Boursault's *Le portrait du peintre*, the same line is cited and the ridiculous Count claims that the line is directed against Ama-

18. The more global sense of "l'école des femmes" is supported by Lisette's ending lines in *L'école des maris*: "If any husband is a churlish fool, / This is the place to send him—to our school" (Molière, *Tartuffe and Other Plays*, tr. Donald Frame [New York: Signet Classics, 1967], 89). On "docile bodies," see Michel Foucault, *Surveiller et punir: Naissance de la prison* (Paris: Gallimard, 1975), 157–62.

19. *L'école des femmes*, 2.5.603–06 (27).

20. Ibid., 5.4.1527 (61). In the original: "Le moyen de chasser ce qui fait du plaisir?", a more literal translation of which might read, "How can you get rid of that which gives you pleasure?"

21. *Zélinde*, 64.

rante, who replies: "Not that it matters to me; / But the author is mighty bold to treat me this way. / He owes me respect."[22]

In *La critique de l'École des femmes*, Molière had already sought to defuse any such efforts to turn Arnolphe into the spokesperson for the author, but his efforts to distinguish between character and author fell on deaf ears. Robinet has Crysolite "defend" Molière from accusations that he is trying to keep women locked up and ignorant by insisting that there is nothing reprehensible in Arnolphe's maxims, concluding, "As for me, I would have no problem sending my wife to hear such a sermon and to place it in her hands to study; and I wouldn't choose anything better for her instruction, being convinced that, provided she keep these maxims well in mind, she will be a respectable wife and no coquette."[23] Crysolite's apology for Molière comes down in favor of tyrannical patriarchy, and conveniently forgets that the entire plot and tenor of *L'école des femmes* serves to make Arnolphe and his views ridiculous. When Crysolite eventually reveals that he was only pretending to hold such abhorrent views regarding women in order to enliven the conversation, the play ends with all the characters roundly condemning the reprobate views of Molière, who dares to suggest that women be kept from writing, parties, or socializing—the very views that Molière had criticized in his play.

Most surprising of all is La Croix's *La guerre comique*, in all other respects a fine justification of Molière's play. Regarding the maxims, however, La Croix defends Molière in a manner entirely adverse to the original play's intention. When Rosimon attacks Arnolphe's maxims as "pernicious," Philinte responds ironically: "Yes, I've always criticized those maxims, they're very pernicious, and husbands should make sure that their wives don't follow them. I have no doubt that you give yours some that are entirely opposite of the ones Molière teaches in his school."[24] Philinte then continues by altering a few choice words in the maxims so that they invert the sense of Arnolphe's, reciting, for example:

When a woman, duly wed,
Comes to share her husband's bed,
She must keep one thing in mind:

22. *Portrait du peintre*, 130.
23. *Panégyrique de l'École des femmes*, 215.
24. La Croix, *La guerre comique*, in *La querelle*, vol. 2, 440.

Following the trend she'll find
He doesn't keep her for himself,
But welcomes all mankind.[25]

La Croix argues, in effect, that there is nothing wrong with Arnolphe's precepts; this is a curious position at best since Molière himself would have disagreed. While La Croix is thus perhaps absolving Molière from accusations of impiety, claiming that Arnolphe's preaching is actually in line with seventeenth-century norms, he overlooks the fact that Molière's play actively undermines these principles. Neither among Molière's enemies nor his allies do we find a single writer in the *querelle* who argues that Arnolphe's principles are antithetical to those of the play's implied author. If the collapsing of the dramatic distance between Arnolphe and Molière is useful for the playwright's critics, who can therefore argue disingenuously that Molière is retrograde in his views on women's liberties, the claim appears ludicrous to any careful reader of the play, and its adoption even by Molière's supporters is perplexing.

In this respect, Bélise's insightful remark cited above regarding the theatrical reaction to Molière becomes even more significant, since genre and morality are operating in similar ways in the quarrel. The productions of Molière's rivals do not only respond to his in form, but they also agree with him on the essential ethics of theater: the celebration of freedom and pleasure that reflected the cultural sophistication of theatergoers. From this perspective, Molière's opponents are at heart merely his rivals, competing against him while sharing many of the same ideological and artistic assumptions. Against the backdrop of such collusion, no intense questioning of theater's aims could be expected. The anti-Molière camp in the *querelle* could argue that *L'école des femmes* was a bad play by neo-Aristotelian standards; what they could or would not do is call into question the moral worldview of theater itself.

It is in this paradoxical sense, perhaps, that McBride's argument of causality best holds up to scrutiny. If the *querelle de L'école des femmes* did push moralists and ecclesiastical authorities to advocate for the complete suppression of theater, it was not because Molière's polemical adversaries, with high moral dudgeon, pointed

25. Ibid., 441. My translation here follows Donald Frame's rendition of the original maxim (*Tartuffe and Other Plays* [New York: Signet Classics, 1967], 128), but with the changes introduced by La Croix.

out the obscenity of his plays, but because they themselves fell back on a strategy of imitation rather than critical distancing. From this perspective, the *querelle* represents the failure of theater to police itself.

Further support of McBride's and DeJean's claims for the long-lasting implications of the *querelle* can be found in the texts of the later and larger debate regarding theater's morality. While the abbé d'Aubignac in his *Dissertation sur la condamnation des théâtres* (1666) describes a general theatrical decadence, writers like the Sieur de Rochemont, in his *Observations sur une comédie de Molière intitulée Le festin de pierre* (1665), hold Molière singly responsible for the current moral turpitude of the stage:

> All of France is indebted to the late Cardinal de Richelieu for having purified the theater and trimmed away all that could shock modesty or offend chaste ears; he reformed even the clothes and gestures of this courtesan and came close to making her honorable. Virgins and martyrs appeared on stage, and modesty and faith were made to sink imperceptibly into the soul with pleasure and joy. But Molière ruined everything that this wise leader had ordained regarding theater, and he turned a virtuous girl into a hypocrite.[26]

The Prince de Conti, the former drama-loving rake and sponsor of Molière's troupe who had subsequently undergone a religious conversion, writes in his virulently anti-theatrical *Traité de la comédie et des spectacles* (published posthumously in December 1666): "There is nothing more scandalous than the fifth scene of the second act of *L'école des femmes*."[27] And of course Molière's life, works, and death will still be prominent enough in 1694 for Bossuet to use the playwright and actor's bad end as a moral exemplum in his refutation of Caffaro's laxist views.[28]

However, it is not the persistent citation of Molière in the broader quarrel over the morality of the theater that provides the most compelling argument for continuity between it and the brief comic war. If we look for the most insightful readers of *L'école des femmes*—that

26. In Molière, *Œuvres completes*, ed. Georges Couton, vol. 2 (Paris: Gallimard, 1971), 1201–02.

27. Armand de Bourbon, Prince de Conti, *Traité de la comédie et des spectacles*, ed. Karl Vollmöller (Heilbronn: Verlag von Gebr. Henninger, 1881), 32.

28. Jacques-Bénigne Bossuet, *Maximes et réflexions sur la comédie* (Paris: Jean Anisson, 1694), 19–20.

is, those who most astutely understood the stakes of Molière's play—they are not to be found among Boursault, Donneau de Visé, and their ilk. In this respect, only the moralists such as Conti or Rochemont, who writes after the initial quarrel had run its course, appear to be worthy interlocutors of Molière, demonstrating in their admittedly unfriendly readings a firm understanding of the principles that the play espouses. While a writer like Rochemont exaggerates the moral effects of *L'école des femmes*, he can at least be given credit for seeing that Molière's comedy ridicules conservative constructions of the feminine instead of supporting them: "The naivety of his Agnès has corrupted more virgins than the most licentious writings . . . and more women have become debauched at his school than were lost formerly at the school of that philosopher who was banished from Athens and who boasted that no one left his lecture chaste."[29] For Rochemont, the chief concern is the play's central dynamic: the satire of traditional gender roles and theater's capacity to teach new and controversial models of behavior. Molière's "famous schools of impurity" spread into the souls of their viewers "those dire poisons that extinguish modesty and shame."[30] Their principal role, then, is to "train coquettes" and to "provide dangerous instruction to girls."[31]

Moreover, the corruption of women is linked to the celebration of passion and the ethics of pleasure that justify this passion. Conti writes, "It is true that the goal of theater is to move the passions, as those who have written about poetics agree; and on the contrary, the entire goal of Christian religion is to calm them, pull them down, and eliminate them as much as possible in this life."[32] From this perspective, Molière's play is particularly suspect, since "moving the passions" is not only the meta-theatrical goal of the play itself, but also constitutes the immediate objective of its two chief male rivals, as the final act makes clear. After Horace unwittingly entrusts Agnès back to the care of her tyrannical guardian, Arnolphe interrogates her regarding her feelings. Agnès admits that she loves Horace and not Arnolphe, and upon Arnolphe's angry response, she asks, "Good gracious! Why on earth put all the blame on me? / And why not make yourself as lovable as he? / I never stopped you trying."[33]

29. *Observations sur une comédie*, 1201.
30. Ibid., 1202.
31. Ibid.
32. *Traité de la comédie*, 21.
33. *L'école des femmes*, 5.4.1534–36; *The School for Wives*, 61.

Agnès reduces the competition between the two men to a simple contest concerning which one can make himself more loveable, and in which she disclaims any role. As she states of her falling in love with Horace, "How could I help it? He's to blame, you realize, / And when we fell in love, it took me by surprise."[34] An unthinking and unprejudiced observer, Agnès bears a strong resemblance to Molière's ideal spectator as described by Dorante in *La critique*: "And the rest judge the play the way a play should be judged, that's to say they let it speak to them. They're not prejudiced, or smugly complacent, or ridiculously touchy."[35]

For the moralists, this is theater's trap: by encouraging spectators to stop thinking and to judge merely based on the pleasure that they feel, pernicious moral lessons are absorbed without any countering intervention on the part of one's conscience. Like Agnès, who states matter-of-factly about Horace that "he made me fall in love, and with the greatest ease," Uranie observes, "Personally, when I go to see a play, I only think about whether it got through to me; if I enjoy it, I don't ask myself if I was wrong, or if, according to Aristotle's rules, I ought not to be laughing."[36] The moralists probably would not care much if Uranie ignored Aristotle's rules—as Thirouin points out, most of them were Platonists anyway[37]—but they certainly would have minded very much if Uranie were likewise leaving out other criteria, namely religious or moral ones, in favor of examining whether or not "it got through to me" (more literally translated as "if it touched me"). The transmutation from the *le* scene's corporeal innuendo "he took my" to a theatrical aesthetics of pleasure is here complete: both Agnès and Uranie may question those who seek to restrict their enjoyment—"How is it harming you?"—while hinting at the futility of opposing pleasure.[38] Just as a logic of definitions and constraint connects the moral critiques of Molière's play with attacks on its theatrical form, Molière's defense in both instances rests instead on individual subjectivity, and on a pleasure that has no need for intellectual justification.

34. Ibid., 5.4.1524–25; *The School for Wives*, 61.
35. *The School for Wives Criticized*, 86.
36. *L'école des femmes*, 5.4.1540; *The School for Wives*, 61; *The School for Wives Criticized*, 96.
37. *L'aveuglement salutaire*, 50.
38. *L'école des femmes*, 5.4.1529; *The School for Wives*, 61.

If Molière's first opponents, those of the *querelle de l'École des femmes*, accurately perceived the threat to genre posed by his new "monstrous" comedy, their responses as often as not sought to exploit similar techniques and appeal to the same enjoyment that had made a star out of Molière. Only the moralists engaged deeply with the larger ethical issues that the play posed—although they left behind the comic quarrel's specific focus on the individual play to undertake a criticism of the entire art form, thus ironically fulfilling to some extent the jeremiads of certain Molière critics: that he would bring about the general ruin of theater. As the conversation shifts, so does the slippage of *comédie* from the individual works and style of Molière to its broadest and most inclusive sense. The unusual assemblage of arguments mobilized by Molière's opponents comprises a discursive policing of boundaries threatened by the ambiguous Gordian knot posed by *L'école des femmes*. The playwright's antagonists, whether theatrical rivals or moralists, quite correctly saw in the play something akin to Agnès's letter wrapped around a rock: a missive that was also a missile, an individual play that argues in favor of an uninhibited natural style and pleasure, and that consequently takes aim at the seventeenth-century constraints placed on both gender and genre.

HALL BJØRNSTAD

"Avec confusion j'ai vu cent fois tes feintes": Imperial Spectatorship in *Le véritable Saint Genest*

The play-within-a-play structure of Jean Rotrou's *Le véritable Saint Genest* (1647) places the spectator in front of two different spaces and two different plots: on the external stage, a wedding plot at the court of the Roman emperor Dioclétian, and on the internal stage, a martyr drama staged by Genest and his troupe as part of the wedding celebration. If all we had of *Le véritable Saint Genest* were the action of the internal stage, there would be no loose ends. The story of the eponymous hero would clearly have held center stage. It would have focused our attention on the greatest actor of antiquity as he staged the martyr drama of Adrian, reenacting the recent conversion of this former trusted official at the imperial court, and on his own surprising conversion that interrupts the play-within-the-play before it reaches its tragic end, the death of the actor taking the place of that of his character. The play would have been a dense meditation on the nature of conversion and on the power of the sacred to transform the most profane space—the theatrical stage—into a vehicle of salvation.

This is in fact how most scholars approach the play, considering the drama of Genest's conversion as a synecdoche for the whole piece. The most forceful expression of this position can be found in an influential 1993 article by Georges Forestier: the play consists of a central mystery play, formally constructed according to the classical unities and framed by a prologue and an epilogue.[1] Within this interpretation, the main challenge of scholarship becomes one of adequately matching expectations: to reveal and foreground the synecdochic relation between main motif and frame; to show how the prologue and

---

1. Georges Forestier, "*Le véritable Saint Genest* de Rotrou: Enquête sur l'élaboration d'une tragédie chrétienne," *XVIIᵉ siècle* 179 (1993) : 321.

YFS 130, *Guilty Pleasures: Theater, Piety, and Immorality in Seventeenth-Century France,* ed. Harris and Prest, © 2016 by Yale University.

epilogue announce and reflect back on the central mystery play; to expose how throughout the entire play the members of the imperial court operate through a double enunciation where it is assumed that in speaking about their own (pagan) concerns, they are nevertheless always already figuring the Christian revelation at the heart of the play. Such an approach has proved immensely productive in the mapping of structural relations between frame and main motif. At the same time, it exposes the interpreter to a hermeneutic temptation, namely the *a priori* assumption that everything in the play makes sense, that everything comes together, and that all the loose ends necessarily refer back to the same univocal central meaning.[2]

Interestingly, expectations like these are exactly what are at stake for the internal audience within the play at the critical moment when they struggle to understand what happens after Genest's onstage conversion. Just as the modern reader does what s/he can to make the frame of the play conform to the tragedy s/he knows s/he is reading, the emperor Dioclétian does all he can to make Genest's unexpected behavior fit in with the plotline of the play he thinks he knows he is watching. In this article I will suggest that *Le véritable Saint Genest* invites us to think differently about the agency and the agents of the theatrical experience at more levels than we might at first suppose: not only about conversion and the transformative power of the actor's performance, but also, and more profoundly perhaps, about the receptivity, passivity, and illicit pleasures of the spectator. Therefore, I will shift the focus from the drama on the internal stage to that of the internal audience as they prepare to watch that drama. In so doing, I propose shifting our focus from the play as an exploration of the supreme actor of antiquity to what might well have been the supreme spectator: Dioclétian.

Within a reading that focuses on spectatorship, questions of why and how the internal play occurs in the first place take on a new meaning. While it is unsurprising that Genest, as an actor, spends most of the time he appears in the external play on stage either playing or rehearsing the internal play, it is less apparent that the imperial court ends up spending its time in front of another play. At the outset, there are no obvious indicators, beyond the title itself, that the action

---

2. To my mind, this hermeneutic temptation has only once been seriously addressed in Rotrou scholarship, namely in John D. Lyons's seminal article "*Saint Genest* and the Uncertainty of Baroque Theatrical Experience," *MLN* 109 (1994): 601–16.

of *Le véritable Saint Genest* is heading toward the representation of an internal play. In fact, in the first scene of the main play, the action seems to be set up by a quite different plot device, namely that of the premonitory dream. We meet Dioclétian's daughter Valérie, who is troubled by a repeated nightmare in which her father forces her to marry a shepherd. The very first words of the play are an exclamation by her maid Camille in reaction to the authority Valérie gives to the dream: "What! You cannot vanquish such a vain fright?" (1.1.1).[3] "Fright" (*frayeur*) is indeed the right word. Valérie seems terrified: the vividness of the dream and the violence of her father in it remind her of her own vulnerable position, exposed to the "whims" of her father (1.1.22), which are also "the whims of fate" (1.1.72). However, not much of the tension built up through the exchange between the two women remains by the time the play reaches the middle of act 1. We learn that Valérie was at once right and wrong in her reaction to her dream: right, because her father has indeed decided to give his daughter in marriage to a shepherd; wrong, because this shepherd is none other than Dioclétian's newly appointed co-emperor Maximin, just back from a series of heroic exploits in India. Where Valérie had feared the whims of her rash father, she instead finds herself mobilized in his attempts at stabilizing his power after the recent restructuring of the central power of the Roman Empire (to which I will return below). Therefore, as Valérie declares, "My dream is explained: I marry in this great man /A shepherd, it is true, but one who rules in Rome" (1.3.193–94).[4] The premonitory dream seems to give way to a wedding plot as the structuring device of the play.

This is the exact point where the action of the play turns toward theater and the actor enters the stage. As the focus shifts from the

3. Quotations from the play will be referenced parenthetically in the text. English translations are adapted from Lacy Lockert's translation in *More Plays by Rivals of Corneille and Racine* (Nashville: Vanderbilt University Press, 1968).

4. Within the wider plot of the play, there is a typological meaning linked to the figure of the shepherd, as pointed out by many scholars. The metamorphosis of Maximin from shepherd to Caesar not only points back to the early history of Rome, as explicitly stated (1.3.159–60), but also evokes the Biblical parable of the good shepherd, in a way that foreshadows Genest's metamorphosis later in the play. However, such a reading is not entirely seamless, since, unlike what we see in Corneille's *Polyeucte*, for example, the conversion of the eponymous hero has no immediate impact on the other characters of the play. The figure of the shepherd remains unfulfilled, to the frustration of later readers like Sainte-Beuve (*Port-Royal*, vol. 1 [Paris: Eugène Renduel, 1840], 182–83).

interpretation of Valérie's dreams to the preparation of her wedding, the tension released is displaced toward the impatiently waiting Genest, as expressed by the rhyme *aime / extrême* ("love" / "extreme") bridging scenes 3 and 4 of act 1:

> CAMILLE. Thus often Heaven devises everything in such a way
>   That what one fears comes through, without affliction,
>   And what one dreads is in the end what one loves [*ce qu'on aime*].

SCENE IV

> PAGE. Genest waits, sire, with an extreme desire [*désir extrême*],
>   To pay the homage owed your Majesties. *He exits.*
> DIOCLÉTIAN. Let him enter.
> CAMILLE, *to Valérie.* Your joys lacked him alone;
>   Whatever your happiness, his art,
>   Somehow seems needed to perfect it.
>   Procure for us, madam, this entertainment
>   Which you yourself value and find so charming.
>
> (1.3–4.199–208)

Camille addresses Valérie, but what she says serves above all as exposition, making explicit to Valérie—and to us—why theater is what the situation calls for. She responds to the report about Genest's "extreme desire" by reminding Valérie about her own extreme desire for Genest's art. As will soon become clear, this desire is shared by the whole group of notables addressed by Genest through the page as "Vos Majestés" (your majesties): Valérie, Maximin, and Dioclétian. Indeed, Camille's exposition makes explicit what is already implicit in Dioclétian's imperial order, which includes Genest in the action of the play by inviting him on stage. Interestingly, it is thus already in the language of theater that the action turns to the actor. The explicit stage direction announcing the page's exit just before line 204—"He exits"—is immediately balanced by the director of the world stage adopting the language of the stage director, stating in reference to Genest: "Let him enter" (1.4.204).

This turn of events is, in other words, presented as a result at once of serendipity (Genest happens to be there, waiting) and of *kairos* (Dioclétian seizes the opportunity). But Camille's words provide the background of this development at the end of scene 3 when she speaks about divine agency: "Often Heaven devises everything in such a way . . . ." The world is presented as scripted at the very moment when the actor arrives with his scripts, but scripted in a way that makes sense only in retrospect. In fact, this line responds to Valérie's very first words in the play, when she explains the terror caused by her nightmares by observing that "dreams, especially when so often repeated, / Either always or often tell the truth" (1.1.11–12). However, there is certainly a further irony here, although it is difficult to say which way it cuts: it could be the irony of the Christian God whose script is more powerful than that of the pagan gods, or the irony of the playwright whose script is guiding the providence of the Heavens, both pagan and Christian. It might be tempting to prioritize the Christian perspective, in light of what will happen later in the play. It is worth noticing, however, that Camille's summary of Valérie's dream experience seems to describe the thrill that draws the imperial spectators to Genest—and the extra-diegetic audience to the theater—in the first place: "what one fears comes through, without affliction"; indeed, "what one dreads is in the end what one loves." It is tempting, therefore, to see already here the elaboration of a more specific analogy than the obvious one suggested by the structure of the play as it moves from dream to theater as its central metaphor: the juxtaposition of dreamer and spectator, the evocation of a certain dreamlike spectatorship through which the spectator is repeatedly subjected to a possibly nightmarish, fearful affliction outside her control, but which is ultimately pleasurable nonetheless.

The same observation could in fact be made about the opening line of the play. Camille's reproach that Valérie "cannot vanquish such a vain fright" (1.1.1) points not only to the vanity, that is, the unreality, of the spectacle of the dream, but also to a mode of relating to it: the ability and power to vanquish ("savoir vaincre"). This is the language of dominance and sovereignty. Valérie *should* retain her composure, Camille seems to imply, not least since the heavens have blessed her with "such a worthy mind in such a worthy body" (1.1.4). Instead, the dreamer is vanquished by—has had to capitulate to—the force of her dream. It is worth noticing that the formulation leaves some doubt as to the agency of the decision, whether what is at stake is an ability (a "*savoir* vaincre") or the will (a "*vouloir* vaincre"). The lingering question is whether the pleasure provided by the dreamlike spectatorship has its source in the loss of control implied in this abdication.

At the moment Genest enters the stage, it is not at all clear why the happy occasion should call for a martyr drama reenacting Adrian's recent and deeply traumatic betrayal of the groom as part of the wedding celebration. The discussion between Dioclétian, Maximin, and

Valérie, on the one hand, and Genest, on the other, about which play to choose is both nuanced and learned. Recent scholarship has identified all the major arguments in favor of theater from the *querelle du théâtre*, and it has often been stressed that the emperor Dioclétian gives voice to many of them.[5] And yet, although ethical and political arguments are evoked, the ultimate decision is based on purely aesthetic criteria, rooted in an assessment of the imperial spectators' expectations about theatrical pleasure.

From the very beginning of the exchange between actor and emperor, the expectation of theatrical pleasure is directly linked to Genest's art. It is true that Camille in the passage quoted above evokes "this entertainment [*divertissement*]" (1.4.207), where the French expression might suggest the play as a mere interruption of more serious matters, as repeated by Genest himself a few lines later at the end of his first speech after entering the stage: the actors seeking to obtain "something that can let us say / That we have eased you from the great burden of empire / And through the charms of our art / Have rid you briefly of your great concerns" (1.5.221–24). But this effect is achieved only because the *divertissement* is "so charming" (1.5. 208, cf. 223). The play as entertainment is able to "divert" its audience through its *charm*, in the strong sense of the term: through its enchantment, through the spell it throws on its audience. This is the reason why the play can be the crowning event of the imperial wedding. In fact, the occasion somehow calls for Genest's acting: "Whatever your happiness, his art / Somehow seems needed to perfect it" (1.4.205–06).

The boldness of this judgment by Valérie's maid is softened by the doubly modifying "somehow seems." However, the point made is reiterated and reinforced in Dioclétian's first words directed to Genest himself, where Camille's "his art" gives way to "your art" in the following apostrophe:

Genest, I appreciate your pains, and the festivities
Of the happy day on which my daughter is wed to this prince,

5. See, for example, the discussion in Pierre Pasquier's introduction to his edition of the play (quoted here from Jean de Rotrou, *Théâtre choisi: Venceslas, Antigone, Le véritable Saint Genest* [Paris: Société des textes français modernes, 2007], 398–401) and in Yann Robert, "De la moralité des tragédies: Le *Saint Genest* de Rotrou et la Querelle du théâtre," *Papers on French Seventeenth Century Literature* 69 (2008): 573–88, 577–78.

And which brings our joy to such a pinnacle,
Without a trait of your art, would be lacking in something.

(1.5.225–28)

But what exactly is it that sets Genest's acting apart? What is this lack (*défaut*) that makes his participation necessary in order for the celebration to reach perfection? Unlike Valérie and Genest himself, Dioclétian does not stress the function of theater as a mere diversion from other concerns, but rather the pleasure it produces and how it will add to the general joy of the happy occasion (1.5.230). However, when Dioclétian passes from a general accolade of Genest as the supreme actor of the age to a testimony of his own experience as a longstanding and avid spectator of Genest's art, we realize that the nature of this pleasure is rather complex. This brings me to my key quotation and to the unexplored model of imperial spectatorship evoked above:

With confusion I have seen a hundred times your acting
Impose on me, despite myself, perceivable blows;
On a hundred different subjects, following your movements,
I have received from your fervor true feelings
And the absolute sway that you exercise over a soul
Has a hundred times turned me into ice and a hundred others into
    flames.
Through your art heroes, more resuscitated
Than imitated and portrayed
Hundreds and thousands of years after their funeral,
Once more push forward and win battles
And in their mighty names proclaim laws:
You make me, through your self alone, sole master of a thousand
    kings.

(1.5.233–44)

First of all, this is an expression of obsessive spectatorship: "I have seen a hundred times." What draws Dioclétian repeatedly to Genest's performance is the impact it has on him. Each time, he knows that what he is seeing is not real ("your acting"), but nevertheless the force of what he sees on stage ("your movements"; indeed "your fervor") moves him to the extent that he experiences "perceivable blows" and "true feelings," transforming him into ice and fire. This is a bodily experience. If the heroes from the past are not only imitated and portrayed, but also resuscitated, it is because of the reality of Genest's incarnation of their passions: a remote past and a vibrant present merging in the force of these "movements" and this "fire," at once his and theirs. And the spectator's, in his bodily reaction to them that leads to the actor's "absolute sway" (*empire absolu*) over his soul.

It is worth commenting on the syntax of the passage. Three times in twelve lines, we encounter the object form of the first person singular personal pronoun *me*: "your acting / Impose on *me*"; your "absolute sway . . . has . . . turned *me* into"; "You make *me*." The emperor is reduced to passivity and receptivity, and is quite literally acted upon by the actor, as expressed most forcefully in line 234: Genest's play affects him against his will. And yet this passivity is not total. Dioclétian does not quite simply relinquish his imperial agency. This is particularly obvious in the last line of the passage where Genest acts, but only as Dioclétian's agent, contributing to the latter's dominance over "a thousand kings" resuscitated from the past.

Elsewhere in the exchange between the supreme actor and the supreme spectator, surrounding the passage quoted above, we see a complex web of negotiations of agency and sovereignty between the two men. Genest ends his first address to Dioclétian evoking "your great pains [*soins*]" at the head of the empire (1.5.224), only to have Dioclétian immediately returning the favor: "Genest, I appreciate your pains" (1.5.225). Those words are the opening of the emperor's long tribute to Genest's art, of which the passage above constitutes the center piece. Genest's reaction to Dioclétian's praise of his confusion-inducing abilities is cut short by the emperor after only one line, which runs as follows: "This glory, sire, confounds me so much . . ." (1.5.251). The suspension at the end of the line not only evokes an external interruption by the emperor, but also an internal cessation of words. This glory confounds him to the point of leaving him dumbstruck. In this way, these eight words are enough to highlight a double reciprocity between the two men: in the overwhelming *confusion* emerging from their interaction (the "with confusion" (1.5.233) of the emperor confounding the actor) and in the awareness that "this glory" that is bestowed upon him is indeed an attribute of royal power. Here, both confusion and glory point back to "the absolute sway" that Genest seizes over the emperor's soul through his acting (1.5.237). By entering the theater and the contract of the theatrical illusion, by accepting, indeed embracing, the role as passive spectator, the emperor subjects himself to the "empire" of the play. In the case of Genest's play, this empire becomes absolute, and this absoluteness seems to be what attracts Dioclétian: a mirror of the power that he himself commands in the empire outside the theatrical illusion. In one way, the transfer of power between the two empires is absolute, but only within a wider set of transactions of power, praise and pleasure.

Interestingly, Dioclétian praises Genest for his *empire absolu* in a political situation in which he himself has just curtailed his own absolute power over the Roman Empire. As Valérie states in the opening scene of the play when complaining about her father's capricious ways, there are now "over the universe two sovereign heads" (1.1.33), namely Dioclétian and Maximian (not to be confused with Maximin), and in total "four heads to the body of the universe" (1.1.36), since in this new political structure each sovereign Auguste is assisted by a Caesar: Dioclétian by Maximin, and Maximian by Constance. After this radical reform, Dioclétian is now himself governing the Western half of the empire alongside Maximin. "But why for one sole [empire] so many different masters . . . ?" asks Valérie (1.1.35) before complaining that Maximin "seems to steal the laurels from the head of my father" (1.1.44) by his recent military exploits. Dioclétian's answer lies obviously in the wedding plot about to unfold. The geopolitical context of the wedding in which Genest will display his *empire absolu* is thus part of a wider plan to stabilize the power of the father of the bride.

Returning now to the core passage quoted above, we notice the split subjectivity expressed in its opening phrase. There is an "I," an imperial subject that is observing not only Genest's make-believe ("your acting"), but also and even more acutely, its effect on himself: "I have seen . . . your acting / Impose on me, despite myself . . . ." The gaze is in fact split: I have seen myself being passively carried away, filled "despite myself" by true passions inspired by "your acting." There is, in other words, a fascination at two levels. First, obviously, in the theatrical enchantment itself, when the limit between illusion and reality gets blurred; second, and more surprisingly, in the self-centered gaze at the loss of control implied in the "despite myself." Already the first time Dioclétian saw Genest act he was confused— and confounded—by the way illusion and reality merged perfectly. Then he came back for more, ninety-nine more times. How is this obsessive repetition to be understood?

"With confusion": it is important, first of all, to notice that this adverbial modifier pertains to both sides of the split gaze. It not only names the effect produced by the theatrical illusion, but also characterizes the mindset in which the emperor has seen himself absorbed by his own reaction. The confusion is at the core of his fascination. On the one hand, then, the elements "with confusion" and "despite myself" are clearly attributed a positive value in the phrase, as the key expressions of the formulation of the emperor's aesthetics. On the other, as Furetière reminds us in his *Dictionnaire universel*, "CONFUSION also means, Shame,"[6] and I will argue that the sense of shame, a strangely pleasurable shame, is equally present in this passage.

This aspect of Dioclétian's multi-layered confusion can best be understood within the context of a Stoic ideal of self-mastery, as pertinent for a Roman emperor as it was in seventeenth-century France. Pascal provides a staunch formulation of this ideal, when he condemns the loss of control implied in pleasure-seeking sexuality, formulated in the language of sovereignty: "mastery and control [*empire*] alone bring glory, and subjection alone brings shame."[7] But we need not look further than the very first phrase of the play to find a similar articulation of this ideal as Camille criticizes Valérie for letting herself being carried away by "such a vain fright" (1.1.1), possibly jeopardizing her dignity (1.1.4). However, already on that occasion, a certain resistance to the Stoic ideal can be discerned. Pascal's neat dichotomy is undone by an economy of obscure pleasure. Dioclétian is confounded by the nature of his own desire: the attraction seems to reside exactly in Genest's power to unhinge him, and the pleasure in his loss of mastery and agency. Dioclétian's aesthetics is at heart an aesthetics of confusion; what he seeks in the theater seems to be a willing—and willingly shameful—subjection to the mastery of the supreme actor, what he calls "the absolute sway that you exercise over a soul" (1.5.237), in a relation to the actor that borders on what we might today call sadomasochistic.

There is an intriguing intertextual echo in the words through which Rotrou lets Dioclétian describe his reaction to Genest's perfor-

---

6. Antoine Furetière, *Dictionaire universel* (La Haye: Leers, 1690), s.v. "confusion."

7. Blaise Pascal, *Pensées*, trans. Roger Ariew (Indianapolis: Hackett, 2005), fragment 648. Ariew follows Philippe Sellier's ordering of the fragments.

mance in his long speech. Whereas the spectator appearing through this portrait is nothing like the theoretical models of spectatorship implicit in the writing on theater from the period, it recalls the way Guez de Balzac evokes his experience as the spectator of Mondory, celebrated as the greatest French actor of the 1630s (if not the whole century) and compared by both Balzac and Corneille not to Genest but to that other Roman epitome of superb acting, Roscius. The following two passages are quoted from the famous letter Balzac wrote to the actor himself in 1636, celebrating his most recent triumph as Hérode in Tristan L'Hermite's *La Mariamne*, while his even greater triumph as the eponymous hero in Corneille's *Le Cid* followed a few months later. Balzac refers to Mondory's consistent impact on his audience ("us"), and in the second passage more specifically to his Hérode, refusing the humility expressed by Mondory in this regard in an earlier letter:

> For you indeed make us see past greatness and magnificence so highly that one must admit that your representations are glorious resurrections of the princes you are representing.
>
> But although you humble yourself, you cannot erase from my memory this first image of majesty that you left there; and I cannot picture you in my mind but with a commanding tone and the eloquence of a master so elevated above this inferior rhetoric that operates only by prayers and reprimands.[8]

At a superficial level, the clearest resonance from this text in Rotrou's play is probably the idea that the supreme actor somehow brings back to life the heroes from a remote past, as pointed out by Pierre Pasquier in the introduction to his edition of the play.[9] However, I would claim that the real importance of the juxtaposition is elsewhere, namely in the way the case for such a perceived resurrection is made. In both texts, the excellence of the actor is established through a language and grammar of sovereignty. We realize from the passages from Balzac that there is something imposing in Mondory's acting, something that is stronger than both men, expressed already at the level of the agency of the phrase: "one must admit that," "you cannot [*ne sauriez*]," "I cannot [*ne saurais*]." Indeed, the real presence of a resurrected past imposes itself on the audience, as conveyed through a language of superiority ("greatness," "magnificence," "glorious,"

8. *Les œuvres de Monsieur de Balzac* (Paris: L. Billaine, 1665), vol. 1, 419–20.
9. Pasquier, Introduction [to *Le véritable Saint Genest*], n. 99, p. 401.

"majesty," "commandment," "master"), if not of excessive superiority ("so highly," "so elevated").

Like Dioclétian's Genest in Rotrou's play, Balzac's Mondory thus seems to incarnate sovereignty in a way that exerts an all-imposing *empire absolu* on the audience. Whether or not there is a direct influence from Balzac to Rotrou, this juxtaposition serves to identify a way of thinking about spectatorship, a way of perceiving a certain kind of supreme acting in the 1630s and 1640s. The perception of excellence in acting is linked not only to the power of blurring the line between illusion and reality (confusion), but also somehow to certain roles and a way of quite literally dominating or commanding not only the stage but also the spectators. As Balzac's formulation makes clear, what we are talking about is not simply the "resurrection" of the ancient prince, but the "*glorious* resurrections." Mastery in acting is linked to the display, indeed the incarnation, of majesty in the enactment of past heroes. The ancient hero is brought back to life in all his glory, in all his public dignity, and the reaction of the supreme spectator seems to be solicited by this glorious resurrection. At the same time, this is certainly a two-way process, the "confused" reaction of the sovereign spectator not only confirming the glorious dignity of the performed character, but also somehow conveying a certain majesty to the performance and performer.

This is paradoxical for at least two reasons, first because of the traditional perception of the *indignity* of the acting profession (not only at the time of Mondory, but also in Genest's day), and second because of the early seventeenth-century differentiation of private zeal and public disinterested dignity on which the absolutist solution of the post-religious wars era was grounded. Hélène Merlin-Kajman spells out the full implications (and imbrication) of these two paradoxes, by exploring how the tragic actor "performs precisely those passions whose elimination the underlying movement of history is prescribing at that very same moment."[10] Her case in point is none other than Mondory, in his relation to the supreme spectator of the age, namely Richelieu.[11] There is in fact a history of mutual admiration between

10. Hélène Merlin-Kajman, *L'absolutisme dans les lettres et la théorie des deux corps: Passions et politique* (Paris: Champion, 2000), 113–14.
11. Richelieu's place as the supreme spectator of the age is of course immortalized by Corneille in his dedicatory letter to the cardinal in *Horace* (1640), where the playwright describes reading the signs of pleasure on the cardinal's face as the absolute

Richelieu and Mondory, leading to private readings by the actor for the cardinal, the favor returned by tears from the cardinal, an eventual royal pension, etc. As in Rotrou's play, there seems to be a link between the mirroring of the sovereign's predicament onstage and the transactions of sovereignty between stage and spectator. Richelieu, like Dioclétian, normally plays only the role of his eminent dignity, except when he comes to the theater and assumes the role of the spectator. Repeatedly, and with pleasure, he submits himself to the troubling, confusing presence of the supreme actor and his *empire absolu* over his soul. He is moved by his play, affected, in Merlin-Kajman's words, "by the complex representation of mechanisms of sacrifice and of their consequences."[12]

Then the play is interrupted. Both Mondory and Genest lose control spectacularly on stage, while pressing their art and their *empire absolu* over the audience to an extreme. In the case of Mondory, it happens when he returns to the role of Hérode after the triumph as Rodrigue in *Le Cid*, hit by a stroke that paralyzes his tongue and right hand at the moment of highest fury in his final curse against the Jewish people: "Run plunging daggers into my heart."[13] And it happens to Genest while playing the role of Adrian as part of the imperial wedding celebration, when he radically confuses shirt and skin, converting to Christianity and suffering the martyrdom of his character, in a process that begins already while rehearsing the internal play, with the three times repeated exhortation by the character of Adrian to himself: "You, give your throat to the knife, see your blood flow / And die without trembling, standing, and according to your rank." (2.2. 343–344; 2.2.347–348; 2.7.485–86). In both cases the reflexive language of the character spills over and reflects the actor's circumstances. The "my heart" offered for stabbing by Hérode beats under the skin of Mondory. The "you" of Adrian's apostrophe to himself addresses the actor who at that moment incarnates him and no longer just represents him.

---

verdict about the quality of the performance. See Corneille, "Épitre à Monseigneur le Cardinal duc de Richelieu" [dedicatory letter to *Horace*], cf. Corneille, *Théâtre*, vol. 2 (Paris: GF Flammarion, 1980), 286.

12. Merlin-Kajman, *L'absolutisme dans les lettres*, 114.

13. *La Mariane*, V.2. 1606 (quoted here from Tristan L'Hermite, *La Mariane* (Paris: GF Flammarion, 2003)). See Merlin-Kajman's penetrating analysis of the play in chapter 5 of *L'absolutisme dans les lettres*.

From the perspective of their audiences, then, both actors lose control, while pretending to do exactly that. They lose control, so to speak, by succeeding too well at it: the resurrection of the character that so impressed Balzac and Dioclétian comes at the cost of the actor's life. Therefore, it would be tempting to see a second meaning in Dioclétian's words close to the end of the play when he points out that the intransigent Genest does not really deserve the emperor's mercy since it would be to grab from the actor-martyr's hand "the dagger with which he pierces his chest" (5.6.1694). That dagger recalls not only the weapon of the Christian martyr, but also of Hérode, Mondory, and Genest. It is the dagger with which the supreme actor should have only pretended to pierce his own chest. We now realize that Dioclétian's masochistic pleasure from seeing, "with confusion" (1.5.233), his own passionate passivity and powerlessness arises from his fascination for the nightmarish movement of this dagger between illusion and reality, from the shirt to the skin of the actor. And it is the same fascination that makes him so slow in realizing that Genest has actually lost control of his acting—rather than just pretending to do so—at the end of act 4.

Dioclétian comes to realize that the internal play has gone awry 140 lines after Genest's first transgression of theatrical decorum. The imperial spectator's slowness is often read from the perspective of the Christian audience of the 1640s: it adds to the pleasure of the external audience to know the meaning of Genest's confusion while watching an internal audience on stage that does not. Within the model of imperial spectatorship constructed by the play, this slowness takes on a different meaning. The period of Dioclétian's blindness and the audience's awareness lasts from the moment Genest uses the name of a fellow actor and then his own name instead of those of their characters—"Ah, Lentule! . . . Adrian has spoken, Genest speaks in turn!" (4.5.1243; 1246)—until the following reaction by Dioclétian to Genest's increasingly violent profanation of the pagan gods:

> DIOCLÉTIAN, *rising.* Oh, atrocious blasphemy! Oh, impious sacrilege,
> And for which we will respond if his blood does not atone for it!
>   *To Plancien.*
> Prefect, take care of this and end the actions
> Of this insolent man with a bloody act
> Which will satisfy the hatred of the angry gods
>   *All rise.*

He who lived in the theater expires on stage
And if anybody else, seized by the same blindness
Shares in his crime, let him share his punishment.

(4.7.1383–90)

Significantly, it is not until Dioclétian gets up from the spectator's seated position that he reclaims his sovereignty and acts in his own right. Until that point, he had interpreted Genest's break with decorum first as a sign of the ultimately sublime performance ("See with what art Genest can today / Go from another's guise to his feelings" (4.5.1263–64), then as a lack of theatrical quality (to the whole troupe: "Your disorder finally exhausts my patience" [4.7.1319]).

Sitting down to watch the play, Dioclétian has willfully entered into a contract that suspends his sovereignty, a suspension whose goal is to access the pleasurable experience of captivity under the *empire absolu* of the supreme actor. In fact, this suspension is figured twice in the décor of the play: in the internal spectators' lower, seated position, and in the two prisons onstage. Getting up, Dioclétian suspends the suspension of his sovereignty, so to speak, and reverses the roles of captive and capturer. Importantly, however, he does so while insisting on theatrical metaphors, just as he did while Genest entered the action three acts earlier ("Let him enter" [1.4.204]). The supreme actor will "expire on stage" (4.7.1388); the action will be closed by "a bloody act" (4.7.1386).

In closing, I would like to return one last time to my title: "Avec confusion j'ai vu cent fois tes feintes" [With confusion I have seen a hundred times your acting] (1.5.233). The theater audience listening to this expression of the emperor's guilty pleasure might notice a homophony present in "cent fois" where a "sans foi [*without faith*]" also resonates. At the hundred and first occasion, when Genest loses control of his acting, Dioclétian, the imperial spectator, gets up and insists on playing the role of imperial stage director in order to make sure that we remain within the realm of theater, of illusion. In the end, Genest's conversion remains a "blindness," a confusion of roles, still "acting," still within the "hundred times." The great actor's sublime last performance was lost on the emperor who still did not convert. Perceived by the imperial spectator to be *without faith*, Genest's final performance ultimately fails to convince. What does this tell us about the power of theatrical illusion and the *querelle du théâtre*? As Jennifer Herdt has shown in her study of European Jesuit theater, the love–hate relationship with the stage boils down to a paradox: theatrical illusion is powerful enough to lead people astray, but never sufficient to effect a conversion.[14] However, what Rotrou shows through the model of imperial spectatorship explored here is that the theater's failure to persuade is to some extent irrelevant because sovereignty itself is unthinkable outside the metaphors that the theater provides.

14. Jennifer A. Herdt, *Putting On Virtue: The Legacy Of The Splendid Vices* (Chicago: University of Chicago Press, 2008).

NICHOLAS HAMMOND

"Quel funeste poison?" Racine, Nicole, and Theatrical Crisis

The starting point of this article will be one small corner of the *querelle du théâtre*, namely the response by Jean Racine to Pierre Nicole's condemnation of the theater and the subsequent reaction of two supporters of Port-Royal.[1]

"EMPOISONNEURS PUBLICS": DANGEROUS DRAMATISTS

In the barbed debate between Pierre Nicole and Jean Desmarets de Saint-Sorlin, Nicole turned his sights upon Desmarets's previous work as a dramatist. Retitling his series of letters (letters XI-XVIII) *Les visionnaires*, the Port-Royal moralist chose deliberately to evoke Desmarets's most notable comedy *Les visionnaires*, first performed in 1637 and restaged at regular intervals in 1665–56.[2] In the most colorful passage from Letter XI, Nicole manages to tar all dramatists and novelists with the same brush of corruption and danger:

> A creator of Romances and a poet of the theater is a public poisoner,
> not of bodies but rather of the souls of the faithful; such a writer must

1. See in particular Henry Phillips, *The Theatre and its Critics in Seventeenth-Century France* (Oxford: Oxford University Press, 1980) and Laurent Thirouin, *L'aveuglement salutaire: Le réquisitoire contre le théâtre dans la France classique* (Paris: Honoré Champion, 1997). For an excellent reading of poison in *Phèdre*, see Amy Wygant, "Medea, Poison, and the Epistemology of Error in *Phèdre*," *Modern Language Review* 95/1 (January 2000): 62–71. Although Wygant looks at Racine's part in the theatrical polemic, she does not consider the role played by Desmarets de Saint-Sorlin, Goibaud du Bois, and Barbier d'Aucour.
2. The first ten *Lettres imaginaires* were published between January 1664 and November 1665; the remaining letters, published under the title *Les visionnaires, ou seconde partie des lettres sur l'Hérésie imaginaire, contenant les huit dernières*, were published in 1667.

YFS 130, *Guilty Pleasures: Theater, Piety, and Immorality in Seventeenth-Century France*, ed. Harris and Prest, © 2016 by Yale University.

believe himself guilty of an infinite number of spiritual homicides, either effectively caused by him or caused by his pernicious writings. The more care he has taken to cover with a veil of civility the criminal passions that he describes in his works, the more he has made those passions dangerous and liable to corrupt simple and innocent souls. These kinds of sin are just as terrifying as they persist at all times, because such books do not perish but spread at all times a venom that grows and increases through the ill effects that they continue to produce in those who read them.[3]

The sustained image of the profession of playwright and novelist as poisoner of the public's body and soul seems aimed to provoke the most vigorous response from Desmarets, the self-appointed scourge of Jansenism. Yet, somewhat surprisingly, Desmarets appears in his response both to distance himself from his former profession and to accept the charge of poets as poisoners, telling Nicole that "I have never adopted the profession of poet, creator of theater and romances, or of public poisoner," adding that "thanks to God, in day-to-day life I have other duties than those."[4] Although to modern eyes it would seem strange for Desmarets, who achieved considerable theatrical success, to claim not to have "adopted the profession of poet," we should not forget that in the seventeenth century it was widely deemed acceptable for an *honnête homme* to write verse and prose, but unacceptable for him to make a career of it.

If Desmarets seemed reluctant to take issue with the image of poison in his response to Nicole, it nonetheless became the major rallying call in the ensuing polemic between Racine and those who entered the debate. Racine wrote three pieces in his quarrel with Nicole and two other anti-theatrical writers and supporters of Port-Royal, Philippe Goibaud du Bois and Jean Barbier d'Aucour. However, only the first of Racine's pieces, the "Lettre à l'auteur des *Hérésies imaginaires* et des deux *Visionnaires*," was published in his lifetime, and

---

3. Pierre Nicole, *Première visionnaire*, in *Traité de la comédie et autres pièces d'un procès du théâtre*, ed. Laurent Thirouin (Paris: Honoré Champion, 1998), 219. All references to texts relating to the "querelle du théâtre" will be taken from this edition; page numbers will appear in parentheses after each quotation. My translation. The translations of *Phèdre* are by Robert Bruce Boswell, as it appears on the Project Gutenberg website http://www.gutenberg.org/files/1977/1977-h/1977-h.htm#link 2H_4_0001.
4. Desmarets, in Nicole, *Traité*, 219.

this was the only letter of the three to which Goibaud du Bois and Barbier d'Aucour responded.[5]

Racine begins the first piece by claiming not to take sides in Nicole's spat with Desmarets (mischievously adding, "I will let others judge which of you two is the deluded one"[6]), before registering his objection to Nicole's use of terminology in his war against dramatists and other writers of fiction: "You could use gentler terms than 'public poisoners' and 'terrible people in the midst of Christians.'"[7] The main thrust of the letter is to satirize those at Port-Royal who seem to hold inconsistent views about theater and fiction. The fact, for example, that the "solitaires" at Port-Royal were depicted in a favorable light by Madeleine de Scudéry in her "Roman history," *Clélie*, seems to have prevented them from condemning that particular fictional work's poisonous qualities. On the contrary, Racine tells them:

> I heard [*j'avais ouï dire*] that you had patiently endured the fact that you were praised in that terrible book. You had the volume that spoke of you delivered to your desert, and it was passed from hand to hand, with all the solitaires wanting to see the part in the text in which they were called "illustrious."[8]

Racine's choice of terminology here is illuminating. Instead of poison being spread, we find gossip and rumor being disseminated. Through gossip (*ouï dire*), Racine himself hears of their reaction to their portrait in *Clélie*, and similarly, the book is passed from person to person at Port-Royal itself, like a rumor being spread. Immediately after these lines, Racine again writes about "the rumor that was spreading,"[9] this time referring to the false rumor in Pascal's *Lettres provinciales* that Desmarets was working on a defense of the Jesuits. I would argue that what might seem like the casual juxtaposition of imagery pertaining to poison and gossip becomes something much more significant in Racine's later theater, especially at the time when he was contemplating abandoning the theater altogether.

5. According to Thirouin, Racine chose not to publish the last two pieces, either on the advice of Boileau or following an arrangement or compromise with Port-Royal (Nicole, *Traité*, 220).

6. Jean Racine, "Lettre à l'auteur des *Hérésies imaginaires* et des deux *Visionnaires*," in Nicole, *Traité*, 225.

7. Ibid., 226.

8. Ibid., 228–29.

9. Ibid., 229.

Another perceived inconsistency that Racine is keen to point out in the light of Port-Royal's hostility to the theater is the fact that one of the leading pedagogues and translators at Port-Royal, Louis-Isaac Lemaistre de Sacy, chose to translate the works of the Latin dramatist Terence. As Racine playfully concludes: "So there you are yourselves in the ranks of poisoners."[10] In their counter-polemic, both Goibaud Du Bois and Barbier d'Aucour, stung by Racine's implication of hypocrisy, sprang to the defense of Port-Royal by developing the very terms and examples that Racine had used. Both profess surprise at Racine's objection to the poisoner label by using the ingenious argument that the passions inspired within the theater are themselves forms of poison. As Goibaud du Bois tells the playwright:

> Perhaps you forgot in writing your letter that the theater has no other purpose than to inspire passions in the spectator, and that the passions, even as seen by pagan philosophers, are the diseases and poisons of the soul.[11]

Indeed, he adds, Racine would seem to be the only dramatist not to accept this premise:

> I think that after you there is not a single person who doesn't know that the art of the theater consists mainly of the concoction of such spiritual poisons. Haven't they always called the theater "the art of bewitching," and haven't they believed that in giving the theater such a quality, they have placed it above all the arts? Can't it be seen that their works are composed of an agreeable mixture of intrigues, interests, passions and people, where what is true does not enter their heads, but only what is appropriate to move spectators, and to allow passions that poison them to flow in their hearts, to the extent that they forget themselves and immerse themselves in imaginary intrigues?[12]

Despite acknowledging that certain lines of dramatic verse might be deemed innocent, Goibaud du Bois is uncompromising in his view

10. Ibid., 228. In his second piece, "Lettre aux deux apologistes de l'auteur des *Hérésies imaginaires*," which remained unpublished, Racine extended his theatrical comparison to Pascal's *Lettres provinciales*, asking, "And does it seem to you that the *Lettres provinciales* are anything other than comedies?" (Ibid., 269). Wygant makes the convincing argument that Racine's spat with Nicole has less to do with defending the theater than deciding who will be the new Pascal: "The object of the discussion is not the apparent subject of the debate but rather rhetorical superiority itself." Wygant, "Medea, Poison," 67.

11. Goibaud du Bois, in Nicole, *Traité*, 228.

12. Ibid., 235.

that "the poet's will is always criminal"[13] and that, even if certain poetic lines lack the requisite power to poison the audience, "the poet always wants his verses to poison."[14]

In response to Racine's comment that Sacy, who had translated the works of Terence, might also be branded a poisoner, both Goibaud du Bois and Barbier d'Aucour leap to Sacy's defense, citing the pedagogical purpose of such translations; they were to be used for teaching pupils at the Port-Royal schools in suitably abridged versions.[15] As Goibaud du Bois asks:

> What link can you find between a theatrical poet and the translator of Terence? One translates an author for the education of children, which is a necessary good; the other writes plays, the best quality of which is to be without use. One works to elucidate the language of the Church, the other learns to speak the language of fables and worshippers of idols; one removes all the poison that the pagans put into their theater, the other composes new plays and tries to put new kinds of poison into them.[16]

Barbier d'Aucour takes a similar position:

> What therefore can one say of the person who, in order to have a pretext to call the author of this translation a poisoner and, according to the new permission that he grants himself, to envelop all those at Port-Royal with such a reproach, tries himself to poison a purpose that is not only absolutely innocent but also very praiseworthy and useful?[17]

The fact that both defenders of Port-Royal set the idea of the "utilité" (usefulness) of Sacy's pedagogical project against the "inutilité" (unusefulness) of the theater calls to mind Goibaud du Bois's biblical reference to the dangers of "paroles oisives" (idle words)[18] when he cites Matthew 12:36, "every idle word that men shall speak, they shall give account thereof in the day of judgment."[19] Such critics seem to

13. Ibid., 245.
14. Ibid.
15. For a discussion of the Port-Royal school's use of selected extracts in the teaching process, see Nicholas Hammond, *Fragmentary Voices: Memory and Education at Port-Royal* (Tübingen: Gunter Narr, 2004), especially 53–88.
16. Goibaud du Bois, in Nicole, *Traité*, 245.
17. Barbier d'Aucour, in ibid., 260.
18. Goibaud du Bois, in ibid., 236.
19. In Sacy's translation, "les hommes rendront compte au jour du jugement de toute parole inutile"; in the Vulgate, "omne verbum otiosum."

apply the status of idle gossip to the theater, in the same way that the 1690 Furetière dictionary defines "caquet" as an "abundance of useless words, lacking all solidity."

POISONOUS WORDS: GOSSIP AND RUMOR IN *PHÈDRE*

Phèdre's theatrical impact needs no biographical or contextual information in order to be fully appreciated. However, the personal and professional crisis that Racine seems to have encountered when he, more or less concurrently, abandoned the theater, started working with Boileau as historiographer to the King, and secretly re-established ties with Port-Royal is significant in a broader context. It is clear that both Racine's preface to *Phèdre* and his son Louis's analysis of the circumstances of the first performances of the play in his *Mémoires contenant quelques particularités sur la vie et les ouvrages de Jean Racine* make a direct link between *Phèdre* and the earlier theatrical debate with Port-Royal, evoking in the process many terms used in that *querelle*.

By stressing the centrality of virtue in *Phèdre*, Racine expresses the hope that the "solid" and "useful" instructions contained in his play might serve as "a way of reconciling Tragedy with a number of people, famous for their piety and doctrine, who have condemned it in recent years."[20] He clearly has in mind here the words of one of these famously pious denunciators of the theater: Nicole had made the point in the subtitles of sections of the 1667 version of his *Traité de la comédie* that "Christian virtues are not effective on stage"[21] and that "the theater has no solidity."[22] Racine would seem implicitly to admit here that his previous tragedies lacked the "usefulness" and "'solidity'" of this new work and to accept, whether for rhetorical effect or from personal conviction, that his previous theater did indeed have the status of idle talk that Goibaud du Bois had applied to it. For his part, Louis Racine is keen to see *Phèdre* as an important transition point for his father between a worldly life and a pious one. As Georges Forestier has pointed out in his edition of Racine's complete

20. Jean Racine, *Œuvres complètes*, vol.1, ed. Georges Forestier (Paris: Pléiade, 1999), 819. All references to Racine's theater and Louis Racine's memoir of his father are taken from this edition. My translation.
21. Nicole, 64.
22. Ibid., 106.

theater, Louis's observation was largely responsible for many subsequent Jansenist readings of the play (1621–26). For our purposes, it is interesting that Louis should claim that his father, having taken issue with the term "poisoner" to describe the profession of playwrights in the original *querelle*, should, at the time of *Phèdre*, accept precisely the same appellation. This acceptance implies that, whereas his previous plays could be seen in such a light, *Phèdre* is somehow different: "He admitted that the authors of theatrical plays were public poisoners, and he recognized that he was perhaps the most dangerous of such poisoners."[23]

While Racine's return to the themes and vocabulary of the theatrical debate in his prefatory writing might not be entirely unexpected at a time when he was about to take a twelve-year absence from the stage, the reemergence of similar terminology within the fabric of the tragedy itself is perhaps more surprising. Yet, as I hope to show in the remainder of this article, everything that is spread (*répandu* or *semé*) in *Phèdre* —rumor, gossip, disease, poison—recalls the profound unease that lay at the core of theatrical debates a few years earlier and that exercise a powerful hold over seventeenth-century discourse. Silje Normand's comment in her study on perceptions of poison in early modern France that "the language of poison and contamination was used not only to denote physical infection from plague or toxin, but also to connote moral and spiritual degeneracy"[24] is crucial here. My aim is not so much to read *Phèdre* in a reductive manner—after all, the play is far too subtle and rich to be bound up within a single interpretation—but to explore how the reappearance of these themes might deepen our appreciation of the play and offer ways in which the theater can become a commentary on itself.[25]

Much of the tragic action in *Phèdre* emanates from, and is sustained by, rumor and gossip. In his preface to the play, Racine highlights both these elements. Racine emphasizes the importance played by both history (as displayed in the work of a Roman historian like

23. Louis Racine, in Racine, *Œuvres complètes*, 1151–52.

24. Silje Normand, "Perceptions of Poison: Defining the Poisonous in Early Modern France" (University of Cambridge PhD thesis, 2005), 19.

25. Many scholars have considered *Phèdre* in a self-reflexive light, most notably Marc Fumaroli in *Héros et orateurs. Rhétorique et dramaturgie cornéliennes* (Geneva: Droz, 1990), 493–518, and, especially with respect to poison, Wygant, who refers to Racine's "professional suicide" ("Medea, Poison," 6) in the light of the character Phèdre's suicide. However, these scholars do not explore the link between the spreading of rumor/gossip and that of poison.

Plutarch) and myth ("fable," as manifest in Virgil's epic poem *The Aeneid*), in his Preface:

> I tried to maintain the plausibility of history, without losing any of the embellishments of myth, which adds greatly to the poetry; and the rumor of Theseus's death, based upon this mythical journey, allows Phaedra to make a declaration of love that becomes one of the main causes of her misfortune and one that she would have never dared make as long as she believed her husband to be alive.[26]

According to Racine, the rumor (*bruit*) that Phèdre's husband Thésée has died is directly responsible for Phèdre's declaration of love to her stepson Hippolyte. Moreover, the journey that Thésée is purported to have been on is itself "fabuleux," meaning not only (as the 1690 Furetière dictionary defines it) "what is false," but also "invented for pleasure's sake." Thésée's journey has been embellished through its retelling. It has therefore become not only rumor but also part of the story-telling that constitutes gossip.[27]

Racine's use in his preface of the examples of Plutarch and Virgil in order to contrast history and myth respectively is of particular interest when we consider the role played by rumor and gossip in each ancient writer's work. In volume VI of his *Moralia*, Plutarch tells the story of the barber who gossips. As Hans-Joachim Neubauer elaborates with respect to this tale:

> As an opponent of the Epicureans, Plutarch disapproves of idle talk. For this reason he also expands upon the story of the barber, and describes with relish other cases in which gossips and rumor-mongers have had to suffer severe punishments.[28]

Yet, the very reason Plutarch singles out such dangerous gossip "intimates the special status of informal talk."[29] As a historian, Plutarch might be distrustful of gossip, but he also recognizes its particular power.

---

26. Racine, *Œuvres complètes*, 818.
27. See Nicholas Hammond, *Gossip, Sexuality and Scandal in France (1610–1715)* (Oxford: Peter Lang, 2011), especially 5–49, for analysis of the role played by narrative in gossip.
28. Hans-Joachim Neubauer, *The Rumor: A Cultural History*, trans. Christian Braun (London: Free Association Books, 1999), 11.
29. Ibid.

In the *Aeneid*, Virgil shows also the dangers of gossip and rumor, depicting the traditional Roman goddess of rumor, Fama, as having multiple tongues and mouths, mouths that are just as capable of swallowing poison, both metaphorical and literal, as they are of disseminating news and gossip. In Book IV, which deals with the story of Dido and Aeneas (a book that Racine refers to in his preface to *Bérénice* as illustrating just the kind of "majestic sadness" that is essential to effective tragedy), not only does Fama announce "fact and fiction indiscriminately," but we are told that "such gossip did vile Fama pepper on every mouth."[30] Yet, it is rumor that charges and changes the actions of those who receive the news. As we saw in Racine's prefatory comments, the "ornaments" of the Virgilian "fable" serve to add to poetic effect. In the case of the character Phèdre, the false rumor of Thésée's death allows her to articulate fully her love for Hippolyte. Regardless of its truth or falsehood, the rumor almost becomes tailored to the needs of those who hear it. To quote J.C. Scott: "As a rumor travels it is altered in a fashion that brings it more closely into line with the hopes, fears and worldview of those who hear it and retell it."[31]

The central characters in *Phèdre* respond in different ways to the rumor of Thésée's death depending on the ramifications that this death will have on both their personal and political prospects. And of course this principal rumor will elicit yet more rumors, such as that of the political danger raised by the presence of Aricie, Thésée's prisoner. This fear is voiced at the very time that Phèdre is informed of her husband's demise by Panope, in act 1, scene 4:

> On dit même qu'au trône une brigue insolente
> Veut placer Aricie, et le sang de Pallante. (329–30)

> 'Tis even said that a presumptuous faction
> Would crown Aricia and the house of Pallas.

Even from her prison, Aricie hears the rumor of her captor's death and her impending freedom. Her conversation in act 2, scene 1 with her *confidente* Ismène raises many interesting issues relating both to traditional Greek perceptions of gossip and rumor and to her political

---

30. Virgil, *Aeneid*, trans. Cecil Day-Lewis (Oxford: Oxford University Press, 1998), IV, 96–97.

31. J.C. Scott, *Domination and the Arts of Resistance: Hidden Transcripts* (New Haven: Yale University Press, 1990), 145.

and personal prospects. Indeed, in all of Racine's theater, the *confidents* are often the principal purveyors of such speculative information:

> ARICIE. Ce n'est donc point, Ismène, un bruit mal affermi?
> Je cesse d'être esclave, et n'ai plus d'Ennemi?
> ISMÈNE. Non, Madame, les Dieux ne vous sont plus contraires,
> Et Thésée a rejoint les Mânes de vos Frères.
> ARICIE. Dit-on quelle aventure a terminé ses jours?
> ISMÈNE. On sème de sa mort d'incroyables discours.
> On dit que Ravisseur d'une Amante nouvelle
> Les Flots ont englouti cet Époux infidèle.
> On dit même, et ce bruit est partout répandu,
> Qu'avec Pirithoüs aux Enfers descendu
> Il a vu le Cocyte et les Rivages sombres,
> Et s'est montré vivant aux infernales Ombres,
> Mais qu'il n'a pu sortir de ce triste séjour,
> Et repasser les bords qu'on passe sans retour. (375–88)

> ARICIA.   'Tis not then, Ismene,
> An idle tale? Am I no more a slave?
> Have I no enemies?
> ISMENE.   The gods oppose
> Your peace no longer, and the soul of Theseus
> Is with your brothers.
> ARICIA.   Does the voice of fame
> Tell how he died?
> ISMENE.   Rumours incredible
> Are spread. Some say that, seizing a new bride,
> The faithless husband by the waves was swallow'd.
> Others affirm, and this report prevails,
> That with Pirithous to the world below
> He went, and saw the shores of dark Cocytus,
> Showing himself alive to the pale ghosts;
> But that he could not leave those gloomy realms,
> Which whoso enters there abides forever.

In this extract, Aricie's doubts about the veracity of the news of Thésée's death (asking if it is an "idle tale") show how rumor is always surrounded by uncertainty, or, to use Keith Botelho's words, how it remains "unverified and ambiguous information."[32] Yet Ismène's

---

32. Keith M. Botelho, *Renaissance Earwitnesses: Rumor and Early Modern Masculinity* (New York: Palgrave Macmillan, 2009), 10.

interpretation of the rumor as demonstration of the gods' benevolence points also to the ancient Greek conception of rumors as messages sent from the gods.[33] As early as the second song of Homer's *Iliad*, for example, we find just such a sentiment: "and Rumour blazed/ among them like a crier sent from Zeus."[34] Nonetheless, the fragility of Ismène's assertion is brought out by the incessant repetition of *on dit* in her tale. All that people can rely upon is hearsay and "rumors incredible," narratives that are both unfounded and beyond belief. Emanating from a rumor, the stories, with all their embellishments, are not unlike the tales that characterize gossip. Significantly, the use of the verbs "semer" and "répandre" shows how the various stories are disseminated: they spread like disease or poison.

The political freedom that Thésée's death will bring to Aricie is accompanied by another, more personal, rumor or piece of gossip, the possibility that Hippolyte is in love with Aricie. It is interesting that the word "bruit" can mean both rumor and reputation, because Hippolyte's reputation as an unfeeling and proud man is rehearsed by Ismène, who plays with the idea that she has seen signs of Hippolyte's feelings even if he has not declared his love openly. Aricie's delight at such an "unverified and ambiguous piece of information" (it is "un discours qui peut-être a peu de fondement" —literally, a discourse that perhaps has little solid basis) recalls the pleasure mingled with uncertainty that is so characteristic of gossip:

> ISMÈNE. Je sais de ses froideurs tout ce que l'on récite.
> Mais j'ai vu près de vous ce superbe Hippolyte.
> Et même, en le voyant le bruit de sa fierté
> A redoublé pour lui ma curiosité.
> Sa présence à ce bruit n'a point paru répondre.
> Dès vos premiers regards je l'ai vu se confondre.
> Ses yeux, qui vainement voulaient vous éviter,
> Déjà pleins de langueur, ne pouvaient vous quitter.
> Le nom d'Amant peut-être offense son courage.
> Mais il en a les yeux, s'il n'en a le langage.
> ARICIE. Que mon cœur, chère Ismène, écoute avidement
> Un discours, qui peut-être a peu de fondement!

(2.1.405–16)

33. See Neubauer, "The Greeks . . . were aware of rumors, and viewed them as a power bound up with the gods: as messengers of the immortal and a divine voice." *The Rumor*, 14.

34. Homer, *Iliad*, Book II, 97–98.

ISMÈNE. I know what tales are told
      Of proud Hippolytus, but I have seen
      Him near you, and have watch'd with curious eye
      How one esteem'd so cold would bear himself.
      Little did his behavior correspond
      With what I look'd for; in his face confusion
      Appear'd at your first glance, he could not turn
      His languid eyes away, but gazed on you.
      Love is a word that may offend his pride,
      But what the tongue disowns, looks can betray.
ARICIA. How eagerly my heart hears what you say,
      Tho' it may be delusion, dear Ismene!

As we have already seen in Racine's preface, the crucial confession scene (act 2, scene 5) arises directly from Phèdre's assumption that her husband is dead. In addition to coming to see Hippolyte, ostensibly to argue for the protection of her young son (for which she needs prompting by Œnone at the beginning of the scene), Phèdre makes use of two rumors, one false (Thésée's death) and one true (Hippolyte's intention to leave) as a preamble to admitting her love for him:

On dit qu'un prompt départ vous éloigne de nous,
Seigneur. A vos douleurs je viens joindre mes larmes. (2.5.584–85)

I hear you leave us, and in haste. I come to add
My tears to your distress.

In a time of uncertainty, rumors and counter-rumors abound, and it is surely no coincidence that Phèdre's confession is couched between two contradictory rumors. Just as Hippolyte assesses Phèdre's shocking declaration of love, Théramène is able to report that he has heard the (to him, improbable) rumor that Thésée is alive. Hippolyte's quasi-forensic insistence on getting to the root of the story betrays both his desperation to allow for the possibility that his father still lives and the difficulty of discerning between true and false rumors:

THÉRAMÈNE. Cependant un bruit sourd veut que le Roi respire.
      On prétend que Thésée a paru dans l'Épire.
      Mais moi qui l'y cherchai, Seigneur, je sais trop bien . . .
HIPPOLYTE. N'importe, écoutons tout, et ne négligeons rien.
      Examinons ce bruit, remontons à sa source.
      S'il ne mérite pas d'interrompre ma course,
      Partons, et quelque prix qu'il en puisse coûter,
      Mettons le Sceptre aux mains dignes de le porter. (2.6.729–36)

THERAMENES. A faint rumor meanwhile whispers
   That Theseus is not dead, but in Epirus
   Has shown himself. But, after all my search,
   I know too well—
HIPPOLYTUS.   Let nothing be neglected.
   This rumor must be traced back to its source.
   If it be found unworthy of belief,
   Let us set sail, and cost whate'er it may,
   To hands deserving trust the scepter's sway.

The reality of Thésée's return and the truth of this latter *bruit* lead directly to the various silences of both Hippolyte and Phèdre that Thésée will misinterpret. For her part, from the moment that Thésée is known to be alive, Phèdre, on the one hand, imagines that her incestuous thoughts will themselves become a rumor, picked up even by inanimate objects and made public:

> Il me semble déjà que ces murs, que ces voûtes
> Vont prendre la parole, et prêts à m'accuser
> Attendent mon Époux, pour le désabuser. (3.3.854–56)

> These vaulted roofs, methinks,
> These walls can speak, and, ready to accuse me,
> Wait but my husband's presence to reveal
> My perfidy.

On the other hand, she realizes that her children will have to face not only the reality of their mother's crime but also the gossip about her (the "discours . . . trop véritable"—literally, the all too true words spoken):

> Pour mes tristes Enfants quel affreux héritage!
> Le sang de Jupiter doit enfler leur courage.
> Mais quelque juste orgueil qu'inspire un sang si beau,
> Le crime d'une Mère est un pesant fardeau.
> Je tremble qu'un discours hélas! trop véritable
> Un jour ne leur reproche une Mère coupable. (3.3.861–66)

>   For my sons
> How sad a heritage! The blood of Jove
> Might justly swell the pride that boasts descent
> From Heav'n, but heavy weighs a mother's guilt
> Upon her offspring. Yes, I dread the scorn
> That will be cast on them, with too much truth,
> For my disgrace.

When faced with the spectacle of his family in disarray, Thésée uses the verb *répandre*, which, as we have already seen, is a term that has already been associated with gossip or rumor in the play:

> Que vois-je? Quelle horreur dans ces lieux répandue
> Fait fuir devant mes yeux ma Famille éperdue? (3.5.953–54)

> Why, what is this? What terror has possess'd
> My family to make them fly before me?

From this moment, the verb itself seems to spread into the speech of all the protagonists. After Thésée has left his tongue-tied son in search of elucidation from Phèdre, Hippolyte takes up the image, this time replacing *horreur* with "poison":

> Dieux! Que dira le Roi? Quel funeste poison
> L'amour a répandu sur toute sa Maison! (3.6.991–92)

> What will the King say? Gods! What fatal poison
> Has love spread over all his house!

If we follow the original punctuation of the first edition, as Forestier does in his Pléiade edition, Hippolyte's "quel funeste poison" is exclamatory rather than questioning. The "Maison" ("House," capitalized in the first edition and thereby given accentuated status) becomes, I would argue, not only Thésée's household but also the house of the theater itself, and in particular that of tragedy.

Hippolyte's next encounter with Thésée, during which he confesses his love for Aricie (a claim that his father chooses not to believe), provokes Thésée's invocation of Neptune to wreak punishment on his son in act 4, scene 3. Phèdre (still ignorant of Hippolyte's love) pleads with him in the next scene to respect his own "blood" so that the metaphorical family bloodline may not turn into the literal spreading of blood:

> Ne me préparez point la douleur éternelle
> De l'avoir fait répandre à la main paternelle. (4.4.1173–74)

> Save me the horror and perpetual pain
> Of having caused his father's hand to shed it.

In addition to revealing to Phèdre the awful reality that Hippolyte is a sentient being who loves another woman, Thésée's response points to his inability to believe Hippolyte's assertions:

Sa fureur contre vous se répand en injures.
Votre bouche, dit-il, est pleine d'impostures.
Il soutient qu'Aricie a son cœur, a sa foi,
Qu'il l'aime. (4.4.1185 –88)

His rage against you overflows in slanders;
Your mouth, he says, is full of all deceit,
He says Aricia has his heart and soul,
That her alone he loves.

The "slanders" that Hippolyte is claimed to have spread have the same uncertain status as that of rumor, for Thésée is unable to distinguish between truth and lies. Furthermore, such words have the deadly effect of poison taking hold within the body, frighteningly proleptic of the actual self-administered venom that will soon end Phèdre's life. Thésée utters very similar sentiments in act 5, scene 3, when he accuses Hippolyte of loving Phèdre, even when confronted by Aricie, who herself dismisses Thésée's assertions as unfounded rumors (d'horribles discours).

Two ultimate ironies remain with respect to the imagery and language used in the play to denote rumor, gossip, and poison. First, the verb répandre returns at the very moment that Thésée recognizes his mistake; yet Thésée witnesses not poisonous rumors spreading, but rather Théramène's tears being shed as he prepares to narrate Hippolyte's death:

Mais d'où naissent les pleurs que je te vois répandre?
Que fait mon Fils? (5.6.1490–91)

But whence these tears that overflow thine eyes?
How is it with my son?

Second, the ancient Greek conjunction of rumor with the action of the gods (as we saw earlier) returns at the very moment when Théramène's describes how Hippolyte is dragged to his death by his terrified horses. The possibility that a god, presumably Neptune, was seen forcing the horses to flee can only be described as an unverified rumor, as an on dit:

On dit qu'on a vu même, en ce désordre affreux
Un Dieu, qui d'aiguillons pressait leur flanc poudreux. (5.6.1539–40)

Some say a god, amid this wild disorder,
Was seen with goads pricking their dusty flanks.

Ultimately, divine intervention remains as ambiguous and difficult to ascertain as any of the rumors that have circulated during the course of the play's action.

It only remains for Phèdre to verify the fact that Hippolyte is innocent, before the metaphor of spreading rumor/poison eventually becomes reality in the poison that spreads through her veins at the end:

> J'ai pris, j'ai fait couler dans mes brûlantes veines
> Un poison que Médée apporta dans Athènes. (5.7.1636–37)
>
>   A poison, brought
> To Athens by Medea, runs thro' my veins.

The fact that Racine's final secular tragedy concludes with such a vivid image of poison has a certain poignancy. In making his departure from the stage, Racine, the "public poisoner," in effect poisons his own theater at the moment when the venom takes its deadly effect within Phèdre's body. An initially insular squabble between supporters and detractors of the theater is thus transmuted into something more profound: the nature of tragedy itself.[35]

---

35. See Wygant, "Medea, Poison," especially 68–71, for an ingenious discussion of "erreur" in relation to Racine, poison, and the theater. We should not forget either that in the years immediately following the first performance of *Phèdre* in 1677, poison and rumors of poison were to exercise an even more powerful and vivid hold over the public imagination with the outbreak of the Affair of the Poisons at the end of the same decade. But that is another story. See Normand, "Perceptions of Poison and Jean-Christian Petitfils, *L'affaire des poisons: crimes et sorcellerie au temps du Roi-Soleil* (Paris: Perrin, 2010).

PERRY GETHNER

Love Plots as Moral Lessons in Biblical Tragedies

Among the complaints against the stage most frequently voiced by its seventeenth-century critics is the prominence of love plots. The concerns most commonly expressed were that the positive presentation of the passions would inspire audience members not only to sympathize with the young lovers, but also to become susceptible to similar passions in their own lives, and that this emphasis on worldly feelings could turn people away from making God central to their lives. This problem was particularly acute in those rare biblical tragedies in which the playwrights invented love plots with no basis in the biblical source and made them central to the action. In this essay I shall discuss three such plays and indicate in what ways these episodes, far from undermining the works' overall moral or religious lessons, actually contribute to them.

It is significant that the hostility to drama crossed theological party lines: one of the leading Jansenist theologians, Pierre Nicole, agreed on most points with the staunchly anti-Jansenist preacher, Jacques-Bénigne Bossuet. The objection to love plots was so strong that some of the theorists, who argued that the mere inclusion of one sufficed to make a play dangerous, were willing to concede that serious plays without them (this often meant Greek tragedy) might be morally acceptable. The notion that plays that depicted love were automatically bad whereas those without love were sometimes good was shared by some of the theater's defenders.

Pierre Du Ryer's *Esther* (1644), one of the rare biblical tragedies to be staged by a professional Parisian troupe in the seventeenth century, is a clear attempt to make a religious subject appealing to a secular audience. To this end, Du Ryer invented two interlocking love triangles: the king and his prime minister are both in love with the title

YFS 130, *Guilty Pleasures: Theater, Piety, and Immorality in Seventeenth-Century France,* ed. Harris and Prest, © 2016 by Yale University.

character, while the two female protagonists, Vasthi and Esther, compete for the hand of the king. But it is only the male characters who speak openly of their amorous feelings, and of those it is only Haman who lets those considerations affect his behavior. Haman's passion for Esther (invented by the playwright) serves as part of his motivation for his sinister plots against the king's life and against the guiltless Jews. However, if love is linked to evil thoughts and deeds in the case of Haman, it has exactly the opposite effect in the case of King Assuérus, whose love for Esther, inspired by her personal morality as well as her beauty, ultimately leads him to become a more just ruler. Even though Assuérus genuinely loves Esther, he makes his decision on whom to crown as the new queen for moral and political reasons, rather than privileging his personal feelings: "This submissiveness, as rare as beautiful, makes you worthy of the throne to which Heaven calls you . . . Grace and virtues have been able to carry you to it."[1]

Whereas in some of his other tragedies Du Ryer ingeniously weaves amorous and political motivations together, the link is far less clear in *Esther*. There is nothing to suggest that either of the female protagonists feels love for the king, though both seek to marry him. Vasthi, a haughty and ambitious princess, enjoys wielding power in the world of court intrigue and bitterly resents the fact that since her divorce no one at court will even speak to her. She is so determined to become queen again that she gives herself only two options: reign or die. She has apparently failed to grasp the fact that she continues to display the same type of behavior that alienated the king's affections before: disobedience and overweening pride. Indeed, in the course of her plea for reinstatement, Vasthi never tells the king that she cares about him. Instead, she accuses him of unjustly repudiating her and complains of her present unhappiness.

Esther, although perfectly willing to marry the king, is constantly worried about the dangers associated with high rank, and on two occasions she offers to resign the position of queen to which she has just been appointed. She says that she has agreed to accept the king's offer of a crown primarily to assist her persecuted people. It is significant that while she constantly refers to the king's love for her, she admits to feeling for him nothing more than gratitude and respect. As for her

1. Pierre Du Ryer, *Esther*, ed. Perry Gethner and Edmund J. Campion (Exeter: University of Exeter Press, 1982), 3.1.761–67. All translations throughout are by the author of this essay.

new rank, she states, "It makes me the first subject of a great king, and by showing me the good things I owe to you, it teaches me all the better how to respect my king" (3.1.758–60).

In what ways can the invented love episodes be said to advance the play's moral messages? In the case of Haman, Du Ryer presents frustrated and jealous love as something nefarious. He suggests that even the minister's most criminal plans to exterminate the Jews of the realm and to assassinate the king are linked to, and may even derive from, his frustrated passion for Esther. However, the fact that the playwright has endowed his villain with envy and ambition as well as love makes his motivations harder to assess. Which of these factors is the primary one? The answer to that question can lead us to judge Haman as utterly despicable or as sympathetic, even tragic. Vasthi's desire to remarry Assuérus, whether or not love is a factor in it, is likewise nefarious, since she threatens to foment an insurrection if she is not reinstated. Her plans come to nothing, but again this unsympathetic character is motivated by a desire for power: "I am a queen; let us die for such a fine title . . . There is no middle position that kings can take when angry fate compels them to descend; the throne or the tomb, all the rest is shameful" (2.1.375–79). The lesson seems to be that a love founded on virtue and selflessness can be beneficial, whereas a love contaminated by sinful passions, such as pride, envy, and ambition, is unacceptable and deserves to be punished.

The next two plays under consideration here were both commissioned for private performance at the girls' school at Saint-Cyr run by Louis XIV's second wife, Mme. de Maintenon. Claude Boyer's *Judith* (1695) is unique among the Saint-Cyr tragedies in that, following the premiere given by the students, it was immediately revised for production at the Comédie-Française.[2] However, since only the latter version was published and no manuscript survives, one can only conjecture as to what the revisions were. My own hypothesis is that the version performed at Saint-Cyr was very similar to the published text, but with the addition of a sung chorus at the end of act 5 to celebrate Judith's heroism; Boyer would presumably have removed it when presenting his play to the professional company. The lack of a choral passage would explain both the abrupt ending and the unusual brevity of the final act. But another hypothesis has been suggested: according to an anonymous critique published in 1695, Boyer

2. Claude Boyer, *Judith* (Paris: M. Brunet, 1695).

originally wrote the play in three acts and expanded it to five acts for the Comédie-Française.[3] If there was a three-act version, it probably did not contain the subplot involving the heroine's frustrated suitor, Misael. Nevertheless, I think that, even if Boyer may have begun with a preliminary sketch in three acts, the finished product for Saint-Cyr was the five-act version.

This question of the tragedy's genesis is relevant because, if my hypothesis is correct, Boyer's invented love plot was featured in the version performed by the students, rather than having been added later to suit the tastes of the Parisian public. Although it might seem counterintuitive to argue that Boyer deliberately added a love interest to a school play, this claim is in fact not hard to justify. First of all, Boyer paints a negative picture of romantic love: Misael is moody and almost pathologically jealous; he repeatedly confronts and denounces the woman he loves; and he refuses to do anything she requests. In this respect Misael differs from the virtuous male protagonists in many of Boyer's secular tragedies, for whom absolute devotion to the beloved trumps political and military considerations, and sometimes even self-preservation.

In addition, Boyer reinforces the message that the girls of Saint-Cyr should strongly consider the option of becoming nuns: Judith, while admitting to a "penchant" for Misael (5.7.1457), does not give in to worldly love. Having vowed to devote herself to God following the death of her husband, she steadfastly refuses to remarry. Although the Jews did not have the equivalent of convents, Boyer presents his heroine's withdrawal from the world in terms that would clearly resonate with a Catholic audience: "You were the witness to my secret pain, great God, when I left ashes and retreated. I left them for You, I return to them for You, and I surrender entirely to my divine Spouse" (5.4.1479–82). There are two other reasons to suppose that the Misael subplot was part of the text performed at Saint-Cyr: it was inspired by a statement found in some versions of the text from the Apocrypha that many men desired Judith, though that did not alter her decision not to remarry; and Boyer had invented an analogous romantic interest in his previous play for Saint-Cyr, *Jephté*, in which the heroine

3. This is first stated in an anonymous pamphlet entitled *Entretien sur le théâtre au sujet de Judith* (1695), and scholars have accepted it as fact. See Clara Carnelson Brody, *The Works of Claude Boyer* (Morningside Heights: King's Crown Press, 1947), 80–89; Henry Carrington Lancaster, *A History of French Dramatic Literature in the Seventeenth Century* (Baltimore: Johns Hopkins University Press, 1929–42), 4:324.

also chooses to reject the man whose suit she has favored and has become a kind of nun.

The Misael subplot serves a number of useful purposes in Boyer's tragedy. First of all, Misael presents an alternative method of freeing the Jewish people: he is a distinguished warrior who commands such respect that he succeeds in rallying the remaining young men of Bethulia to make a last stand against the Assyrians. His failure (his men are routed by the enemy's superior numbers) shows that God's plans trump human initiatives. Secondly, Misael offers an alternative future for Judith; although he is in love with her and she feels affection for him, her renewed rejection of him demonstrates the superiority of devoting one's life wholly to God. Finally, placing Misael in Holoferne's tent as a prisoner when Judith arrives complicates her mission and makes her even more embarrassed by the tactics of deception and seduction that she is forced to employ. To demonstrate that Judith's choice to reconsecrate herself to God is both more difficult and more meritorious, Boyer makes the potential marriage of Misael and Judith appear acceptable, at least in a nonreligious context. He therefore has Misael make the following points: he has always loved her, having originally declared his suit at the same time as Manassès, whom she chose instead; as Manassès's next of kin, Misael should automatically have wed Judith after his cousin's death according to the Jewish law of levirate marriage, though again she refused; Misael is a fitting match for her according to the Cornelian model because he is a brave and able military commander, worthy of the heroine's esteem. In addition, he is strongly committed to his religion, having even managed to convert his friend, the Ammonite prince Achior, to monotheism.

From an ideological standpoint, the creation of the character of Misael allows Boyer to demonstrate the contrast between heroes and saints. On the one hand, the hero relies on his own powers to achieve his objectives, takes initiative, and carries out his plans with resolution and efficiency. The saint, on the other hand, takes action only when directed by a call from God and is forced to obey whether s/he likes the mission or not. Paradoxically, Boyer reinforces this opposition between hero and saint by giving Judith and Misael the same objective of assassinating Holoferne, though for Misael that was not the original plan (he tries to sneak into Holoferne's tent only after his military attack against the Assyrians has failed). By letting Judith succeed in destroying the foe of the Jewish people, while Misael fails, Boyer is sending a clear message to the students at Saint-Cyr: prefer solitude and avoid action in the public sphere, unless explicitly commanded to do so by a higher power.

Curiously, Holoferne is closer to the model of the gallant lover than Misael. He treats Judith with unwavering deference, granting all her requests, offering to honor her in various ways (organizing a formal banquet for her, installing her as ruler of the Jews, and, finally, marrying her). When he threatens to have Misael put to death, Holoferne insists that it is not because Misael tried to assassinate him, but rather because he made slanderous remarks about Judith. The extent of Judith's power over Holoferne is revealed when he admits to his confidant Vagao that he was at first tempted to possess her by force, given his overpowering attraction to her, but that he feels a sense of awe in her presence that leaves him timid and afraid to speak. His respect is likewise shown grammatically: as is customary with heroic characters who are genuinely in love, he invariably addresses her using the formal "vous," though she is technically his prisoner (by contrast, he uses the informal "tu" with Misael, also a captive), and continues to do so despite the fact that she consistently calls him "tu." Holoferne even indulges in the hyperbolic rhetorical device, associated with *préciosité*, of referring to his beloved as his god. While his biblical counterpart declares to Judith that if she makes good on her promise, he will adopt her God, Boyer's character goes further, vowing to smash the gods adored by other peoples, while exalting her to divine status along with her God: "You alone and your God will be all of my gods" (4.2.1098). While the sincerity of his love for Judith is undeniable, he has one moment of ungallant thinking: at the start of act 4, worried that his obsession with Judith is keeping him from thinking about anything else, he considers the option of killing her. But Vagao quickly dissuades him, reminding him that Judith has promised him a bloodless victory and confidently adding that if he declares his love she will surely not reject him.

Boyer's interest in divinely inspired feelings appears most clearly in his portrayal of the heroine. In the Bible, Judith views the killing of the enemy general as a perfectly appropriate mission for her and invokes the example of her ancestor Simeon, who took up arms to avenge the honor of his family and of God. But in the play, Judith tells Misael that she is being forced by a superior power to act in a manner inconsistent with both her character and her wishes. Obedience to the divine behest requires a "violent effort" (2.4.482). When Judith addresses God directly, she declares that she is embarrassed and perplexed by the command. In act 3, while expressing her embarrassment over the success of her seduction attempt, she wonders why God could not have chosen a more dignified manner of saving the people of Israel. Instead of relying on her to use artifice to slay Holoferne, which she deems criminal, God could strike him with a thunderbolt. Her revulsion for the task God has assigned her is so great that she must leave the camp briefly to pray for further divine guidance and assistance.[4] In the following act, Judith's distaste for her mission nearly derails the effectiveness of her seduction. When Holoferne declares his love, she can only murmur, "To what do I see myself reduced?" (4.2.1045), and "I shudder with horror over this" (4.2.1048), before finally announcing that she has no other wish but his. Her natural gentleness and modesty again stand in the way when the moment comes to assassinate Holoferne: unable to strike, she lifts her eyes to heaven, and at once "a holy fury" is instilled in her heart, thus allowing her to proceed (5.4.1418). In the final scene, when she assures Misael that she will henceforth shun pomp and honors and never again wear her finery, she declares, "I am fortunate for having made, in the eyes of the All-powerful, an innocent use of so dangerous an art" (5.7.1477–78). One might wonder whether Boyer intended this as a comment on the play itself, in which he used a potentially seductive and worldly medium to teach spiritual lessons.

Joseph-François Duché de Vancy was Boyer's successor as official playwright for Saint-Cyr. He wrote three biblical tragedies for the students there, of which only the third, *Débora* (1706), contains a love interest. Significantly, the title character is impervious to love; indeed, unlike her biblical counterpart, Débora appears to be unmarried. The addition of an extremely complex love plot was certainly deliberate, given that none was present in his biblical source in which Sisera is apparently unmarried and uninterested in women, while Jael and Heber are already married. Duché's chain of lovers consists of four characters: Axa (an invented character, though the name was borrowed from the Bible) loves her husband Sisara, who plans to divorce

4. In the biblical account she leaves the camp to pray only at night and for tactical as well as religious reasons: she wants to establish a pattern of behavior so that, once she has slain the general, the Assyrian guards will not be suspicious when she leaves the camp.

her and marry the woman he really loves, Jahel; Jahel, however, loves her longtime fiancé, Haber, and he loves her in return.

Duché cleverly links the entangled romantic configuration to two related ideological oppositions, one religious and the other nationalistic. The virtuous characters are steadfast in their commitment to their monotheistic faith, whereas Sisara is indifferent to all religion and Axa has converted to paganism, erroneously believing that her apostasy will secure her husband's affection. This structure allows Duché, in what is arguably the play's most original feature, to link the two definitions of idolatry: excessive and exclusive love for a person or thing, and the worship of false gods. The other ideological clash involves loyalty to country: again the virtuous characters are steadfastly patriotic, while the wicked characters are willing to sacrifice their country for their private concerns. Thus, Axa has betrayed her Hebrew brethren by marrying their principal foe and going off to live with him, though at times she feels some residual concern for the persecuted Hebrews. Sisara, who knows that his lazy and ineffective king will not monitor his activities, uses the army to advance his own objectives. On the other hand, Jahel is just as devoted to her people as she is to her God. Haber is even more exemplary: his tribe, the Kenites, as descendants of Moses's father-in-law, are an ethnically distinct group who have embraced the Hebrew religion, yet Haber remains committed to defending the Hebrew people even when it is not expedient politically to do so. Duché places the personal conflicts within a larger political struggle, in which the Hebrew leaders, after originally capitulating to their Canaanite overlords, change their minds and recall their deposed judge; all these developments are his invention.

Of the four characters in the love plot, Haber is closest to the conventional model of the dashing male lead. Like Racine's young heroes, he is virtuous, courageous, and chivalrous, and his fidelity to his beloved is unshakable. Duché provides a new explanation for the curious alliance he made with the Canaanite in the biblical narrative. In the play, the Canaanite ruler, hoping to subjugate the Hebrews without resorting to military force, has persuaded the senior Hebrew princes to detach themselves from the two leaders whose continued presence in their midst would have preserved their independence: Haber, one of their most brilliant generals, and Débora, an indomitable political and religious leader. Yielding to political pressure, the princes agreed to overthrow and imprison Débora, while alienating

Haber by depriving him of his fiancée Jahel. When they finally realize that the Canaanite king does not really have their interests in mind, they turn against him, release Débora from prison, and recall Haber. But Haber's greatness of soul is not lessened by what he thinks is Jahel's betrayal of him: as soon as he learns that she personally is in danger, he hastens to her rescue. In fact, he has pretended to have his army join that of Sisara for the sole purpose of countering whatever sinister designs the latter might be planning.

Because he was writing for Saint-Cyr, Duché was careful to suggest that Haber and Jahel are in love while not letting them declare their feelings explicitly. Duché further restricts the expression of amorous feelings by not providing Haber and Jahel with confidants. In their two big scenes together, Haber simply tells Jahel that he wants to protect her and her people from a tyrant, that he hopes to earn her esteem by his constancy and devotion, and that he would be delighted to see her become his wife. He is quite insistent about the purity of his intentions: "I hasten to your father, and I will inform him of the noble motive that obliges me to take up arms, and to deserve finally, through the ardor that impels me, the friendship of the Hebrews, madam, and your esteem" (2.2.339–41). At times he speaks in the language of gallantry, as in the scene where he bemoans the temporary separation imposed by Débora: Jahel, whom Sisara plans to abduct, is to be secretly moved to Shiloh for her own protection. Yet he does not let love be his paramount consideration. Indeed, when Débora reminds him that their primary objective must be the protection of the Hebrews, he at once acknowledges that he is committed to God's cause, regardless of whether or not he will be allowed to wed the woman he loves.

Jahel, though she admits her fondness for Haber, always focuses on other emotions and concerns. Having been raised by Débora, who refers to her as "my daughter," the young woman is deeply pious and strongly committed to her duties.[5] When Jahel rejects Sisara's marriage proposal, the only motive she acknowledges is religious: her people's Law forbids them to marry nonbelievers, though she also notes that his willingness to repudiate his current wife would give her concern about his ability to be faithful. When Sisara retorts that

---

5. The invention of a kind of mother-daughter relationship between these characters may have been meant to present an idealized portrait of Mme. de Maintenon as mentor of her students.

Jahel is rejecting him solely because she loves his rival, she neither confirms nor denies it. The episode in which Jahel comes closest to declaring her feelings to Haber is when he is about to leave for combat: she expresses her fear that he may be killed, adding, "I am going to lift my hands toward the God of battles; I will implore Him to lead your steps; but who knows whether I will find favor before Him, whether He will wish to turn aside the blow that threatens you; and whether, separating from you in this place, I am not going to bid you an eternal farewell?" (4.4.1171–76). This corresponds to the conventional scene in which a courageous tragic heroine, incapable of trembling for her own safety, trembles for that of her beloved. But in this case the romantic dimension of the episode is minimized and the religious dimension is highlighted.

Although for most of the play Jahel functions as a political pawn, fought over by powerful men, she finally gets the chance to act on her own and achieve truly heroic status. As in the biblical account, it is Jahel who assassinates the Canaanite general, though Duché makes some important alterations to the circumstances. In the play, Sisara brings Jahel to his tent during the course of the battle, rather than fleeing to her tent after it; he collapses from exhaustion, giving her the opportunity to kill him without resistance, whereas in the Bible he requests a meal, after which he falls asleep; Jahel has been kidnapped by Sisara, who has threatened to either kill her or marry her by force, which gives her a personal reason to take his life, as well as a political one. But Barach, who narrates the victory of the Hebrews and the killing of Sisara to Débora and the other leaders, sees Jahel's act in solely positive terms, declaring that she, "avenging the Eternal, immolates the enemy of Israel under her blows" (5.4.1523–24). In yet another nod to the ideology of Saint-Cyr, Duché makes Jahel very modest about her exploit: after Débora calls her the honor of her sex and of her nation (an idea borrowed from the Bible), and declares that her name will be revered by future generations, Jahel declines all credit: "I am unworthy of the honors owed to our victory; the Eternal deigned to make use of my arm solely to show that he controls the fate of battles" (5.5.1598–1600). By muting two key aspects of her personality (her love for Haber and her heroism), Duché makes Jahel a more proper role model for the charges of Mme. de Maintenon.

If the biblical Sisera is little more than the evil instrument of an evil king, Duché turns him into a more fully fleshed-out character. In addition to his total lack of commitment to his king and to his religion (while he frequently taunts the God of the Hebrews, he never prays to his own gods and seems to ascribe no power to them), he is a poor role model both as a lover and as a husband. Although he is intent on marrying Jahel, he tells his confidant, Sévéi, that he originally courted her only because he thought that her father's great wealth and power would enable him rise up the ranks at the Canaanite court. That his present feelings for her are stronger than that is clear from a number of other remarks he makes to Sévéi: he has instigated the current war solely in order to seize Jahel; he alleges only a flimsy pretext to get rid of his current wife; his violent reaction to Jahel's rejection of him sounds like the ranting of a spurned lover; he declares his willingness to fight a duel with his rival over her, though this will have to wait until after the big battle. Moreover, in an unguarded moment he blurts out that he still cares for her: "She would have made my life happy; I'll make her my slave" (3.5.862). On the other hand, he is a most ungallant lover, since he constantly threatens her: if she does not marry him, he will destroy her land and force all the young people into slavery. As for her, he states at various times that he will kill her, or treat her as a slave, or wed her by force. As a husband, Sisara's record is equally appalling, since he treats his wife coldly, despite her desperate efforts to win his affection, and he does not even inform her of his plan to divorce her until she confronts him with that information, which she has learned from Sévéi. By making Sisara's private life as unethical as his public life, Duché again uses the invented love intrigue to reinforce the play's moral and religious lessons.

Axa, the one invented character in the chain of lovers, is a Hebrew maiden who has renounced her people in order to wed the Canaanite general, in part because of ambition but primarily because she is passionately in love with him. She is one of the very rare apostates to appear in a French biblical play. As already noted, Duché links the two definitions of idolatry in presenting Axa: when she married Sisara, Axa embraced paganism in the hope of securing his love, but since he feels no commitment to his own religion he finds her sacrifice meaningless and continues to feel no affection for her. Indeed, he reminds both her and her father that he never forced her to convert to paganism and that she is welcome to return to the faith of the Hebrews whenever she likes. Duché emphasizes Axa's mental anguish: she frequently feels guilt over betraying her people and her religion, and any time things go wrong for her she is convinced that God is punishing her. Yet, when given the opportunity to return to her ancestral religion, she refuses to do so, convinced that God hates her and is incapable of forgiveness: "I am the worthy object of heavenly vengeance" (3.2.714). Needless to say, Duché intended to convey no such message to his original audience. Even after Axa has scandalized the other characters by confessing her crimes, declaring her hatred for her own people, and vowing to kill herself in order to keep God from sending any further retribution upon her, Débora is still willing to take her back into the fold. She sends Amram after Axa to calm the girl and stop her from harming herself, urging him to treat her gently and assuring him that pardon is possible. It is likewise significant that Axa's punishments are self-inflicted: no one forces her to commit suicide, just as no one forced her to abjure her religion. What prompts her final act of desperation is that she has just learned of Sisara's death, and, despite his ill treatment of her, she is unwilling to live without him. It is not simply that Axa has found no satisfaction in the Canaanite religion; her real deity is her husband, and he has proven to be an unworthy and unreliable object of devotion.

In addition to using Axa to show the fate awaiting apostates, Duché invents another area in which she functions as a negative role model: she is placed in a situation analogous to that of Esther but fails to rise to the challenge. In what was presumably a nod to Racine's *Esther*, composed for performance at Saint-Cyr over a decade earlier, Duché wrote a moving exchange between Axa and her father. Amram implores her to put to good use her position as wife of the all-powerful general who has vowed to destroy her people: she can and should intercede with Sisara on their behalf. Both parental figures describe the horrific carnage that will ensue if the extermination is carried out, and both suggest that God may have put the young woman in her current place precisely in order to protect her people. But Axa, despite some residual affection for the Hebrews and a reluctant admission of God's power, cannot bring herself to perform the act that would redeem her. During her interview with Sisara, Axa does in fact plead for her people. He seems on the point of yielding when she admits that her main concern is to regain his love: "Ingrate! Restore your heart to me, and let them all perish!" (3.6.960). From this point on Axa becomes hysterical, offering to assist in the massacre of the Hebrews and in the destruction of their land, and culminating with the plea that Sisara should murder her if he is unable to return her love: "If I cannot, cruel man, soften your barbarity, don't you have enough of it to snatch away my life?" (3.6.973–74). The playwright suggests that performing a selfless act could have led to her spiritual regeneration, but Axa's idolatry (putting her passion above all other considerations) gets in the way.

In all three plays, love (or desire) is carefully subordinated to higher concerns, though the techniques of didacticism vary considerably in nature and directness. Although most of the love episodes are invented, the new material must fit certain basic criteria. Characters are allowed to marry only if they do so in the biblical source; only those characters who worship or respect the Jewish God are ultimately rewarded; characters whose love is obsessive and bordering on idolatry fail to secure their beloved; all forms of criminality, both religious and secular, are punished severely. The exception to this last point is, of course, Judith's assassination of Holoferne, which she is forced to commit by a divine power. What Du Ryer, Boyer, and Duché count on above all in order to convey the impression that the tragedy is fully compatible with a religious perspective is that God is always present in some form, whether as a providential force behind the scenes, as an issuer of commands, or as someone speaking directly through a prophet. Love crowned by marriage can be integrated into the presentation of the divine plan and, as such, becomes inherently commendable. All three playwrights would certainly have felt that their works were genuinely edifying and so ought not to be subject to the strictures of the anti-theatrical critics. The fact that Mme. de Maintenon authorized the performance of the two plays in this group that were composed for Saint-Cyr would seem to confirm that she agreed with that assessment. While little is known of the initial response to these plays from audiences and readers (though there is documentation of reactions to the Paris production of *Judith*), one may conjecture that at least a certain percentage of them considered the blending of secular emotions and religious message to be a valid enterprise and deemed that a biblical tragedy did not have to be either boring or blasphemous. These plays, which mark a conscientious effort to blend the two basic goals of pleasing and instructing, deserve better than the obscurity into which they have fallen.

THERESA VARNEY KENNEDY

From Stage to Cloister: Madame de Maintenon's Classroom Drama

> And now, clothed in vanity, they place themselves on display in the
> center of the stage, like the sirens described by Isaiah, who make
> their dwelling in the temples of voluptuousness, and whose glances
> are deadly, accepting rounds of applause in return for the poison they
> spread through their singing.[1]

In his *Lettre au P. Caffaro* (1694), Jacques-Bénigne Bossuet condemned
actresses, arguing that performing on stage compromised their modesty. Bossuet's remarks followed the historic 1689 staging of Racine's
Esther at Saint-Cyr—a performance that almost literally brought
down the house in terms of the controversy that ensued. A number
of recent scholars have written about Madame de Maintenon—the
founder of the boarding school for young girls from impoverished noble families—and the notorious performances of *Esther*. For instance,
Vincent Grégoire describes the theatrical production of *Esther* and
the religious community's negative response to it.[2] Julia Prest points
to the fact that while Racine omitted Biblical references to Esther's
sexual attractiveness, the performance of the play by a youthful female cast created a scandal nonetheless.[3] Furthermore, this performance was the first time that an educational institution for girls was
able to attract such a large audience. Prest argues that most of the
criticism—both positive and negative—had to do with the effect the
performance had on the girls themselves.[4]

---

1. Bossuet, *Maximes et réflexions sur la comédie précédées de la Lettre au P. Caffaro et de deux lettres de ce religieux* (Paris: Librairie Classique Eugène Belin, 1881),
10. All translations here and throughout are by the author.
   2. Vincent Grégoire, "Avatars de la pratique théâtrale adoptée par Mme. de Maintenon à Saint-Cyr," *PFSCL* 24 (1997): 35–52.
   3. Julia Prest, *Theatre Under Louis XIV: Cross-Casting and the Performance of
Gender in Drama, Ballet and Opera* (New York: Palgrave Macmillan, 2006), 57–75.
   4. Ibid., 59 and 67.

YFS 130, *Guilty Pleasures: Theater, Piety, and Immorality in Seventeenth-Century
France,* ed. Harris and Prest, © 2016 by Yale University.

One aspect of the discussion that has gone largely unexplored is *Esther*'s impact on the theatrical curriculum after the school was transformed into a convent. The fact that Maintenon continued to integrate drama into the curriculum despite the controversy created by *Esther* is important, because it attests to her belief that theater and moral instruction were compatible. While the performance of *Esther* allowed the Saint-Cyriennes to engage with courtly society, the pedagogical plays—morality plays to be performed by the older girls, and proverbs, dramatic plays based on French maxims for the younger girls—were performed only in the classroom setting and specifically excluded courtly society. The public performance of *Esther* taught Maintenon that young women became particularly vulnerable to moral attack when made publicly accessible to courtly society. For this reason, both proverbs and conversations performed at Saint-Cyr warned women against the allure of courtly society and its pastimes, which were depicted as an opportunity for women, intentionally or inadvertently, to put themselves on display. By encouraging the Saint-Cyriennes to reject courtly society, Maintenon not only tried to make up for her prior mistakes, but also supported the goal of the state to provide future virtuous wives and mothers for noble families.

This essay will demonstrate how conversations and proverbs composed between 1690 and 1710 in response to *Esther* disrupted and challenged the dangerous attitudes that the Saint-Cyriennes developed during the performance season of *Esther*. Although the staging of a biblical drama was intended to move her female pupils to loftier goals, ironically, it was Maintenon's secular pedagogical drama that allowed her to successfully corral the Saint-Cyriennes, because they did not become society women in the end. In fact, eight of the Saint-Cyriennes who had performed principal roles in *Esther* opted to take religious vows: Mesdemoiselles du Pont de Veilhan (who had played the role of Esther) and de Lastic (King Assuérus) became Carmelites; Mesdemoiselles d'Abancourt (Aman) and de Mornay d'Ambleville (Hydaspe) joined the Visitandines; Mesdemoiselles de Glapion (Mardochée), de Bourdonné de Champigny (chorus), Le Métayer de la Haye le Comte (chorus) and Hurault de Saint-Denis (chorus) became Augustinians.[5] In the wake of the *Esther* debacle, Maintenon's classroom dramas instructed the Saint-Cyriennes to seek not only the

---

5. See Maurice Cambier, *Racine et Madame de Maintenon* (Brussels: Durendal; Paris: Lethielleux, 1949), 147.

security and comfort but also the routine found in seclusion from society. Theater was one of the means by which the Saint-Cyriennes learned to take on the role proposed by the founder of their institution in seeking eternal solace in a cloistered life.

In the first section of this essay I will briefly outline the theatrical curriculum of Saint-Cyr, the plot of *Esther*, and the controversial aspects of its performance and themes, as well as the initial reactions to the play. In the second section, I will discuss the themes developed in the proverbs and conversations that constitute a direct response to the *Esther* scandal. My conclusion will suggest some reasons for the occupation chosen by the majority of Saint-Cyriennes who had played a role in the staging of *Esther*, as well as some observations concerning the influence of pedagogical drama on future women's status.

MADAME DE MAINTENON AND EARLY
THEATRICAL CURRICULUM AT SAINT-CYR

In 1686 Maintenon founded Saint-Cyr, a boarding school for some 250 daughters of poor aristocratic families. During the period leading up to the performances of *Esther*, Maintenon and Louis XIV were wary of the traditional instruction received in convents. Instead of employing nuns, Maintenon and the king founded a new community of pious women, the *Dames de Saint-Cyr*, who, like the Ursulines, pronounced a vow of celibacy but did not belong to a religious order. The curriculum at Saint-Cyr included not only catechism, reading, writing, arithmetic, and embroidery, but also music and theater. It was Mme. de Brinon who first introduced theatrical arts into the curriculum, but Maintenon did not tolerate her poorly written plays and operas for very long.[6] Maintenon, who greatly admired Racine, encouraged Mme. de Brinon to have the girls recite lines from his plays. We are told that the girls delivered the lines of *Andromaque* with such passion that Maintenon decided they should no longer act out Racine's published tragedies. She asked Racine to write "a kind of moral or historical poem from which passion is absent."[7] Racine, who had left the professional world of theater after the controversial

6. Mlle. d'Aumale, *Le mémoire sur Mme de Maintenon à Mme de Glapion de Mlle d'Aumale* (Bibliothèque de Versailles, cote Ms F 729), 72–73.
7. Madame de Caylus, *Souvenirs de Madame de Caylus* (Paris: Gallimard, 2003), 94–95.

premiere of *Phèdre* in 1677, could hardly refuse the king's morganatic wife and reluctantly agreed.

Maintenon's belief that religious drama could be morally edifying, at least if it was void of all passion, was still a controversial one.[8] While the religious play had peaked in popularity following performances of Corneille's *Polyeucte*, Desfontaines' *Saint Eustache*, Puget de la Serre's *Saint Catherine*, and Du Ryer's *Esther* in 1643, the genre's very right to exist was called into question in the second half of the century.[9] While the Jesuits continued to compose plays on biblical subjects in Latin for their (male) students to perform for special occasions, Maintenon's attempt to carry on the tradition at Saint-Cyr was to prove more problematic.

For all Maintenon's belief in the virtues of tailor-made religious drama, her experiment involving an all-girl cast was a source of considerable controversy. Maintenon was not prepared for the effect these young women would have on spectators seduced by their unassuming charm. The first performance of *Esther* took place on January 26, 1689, in the presence of the king, his son, and the Marquis de Louvois (Minister of War), among other illustrious personalities. Mme. de Caylus performed the prologue with such charm that Mme. de Sévigné, in a letter to Mme. de Grignan dated January 28, 1689, compared her to La Champmeslé.[10] In a letter dated February 21, 1689, Sévigné described the effect the play had on the highly selective audience and on the king himself:

> I cannot tell you how much I enjoyed this play: it is a play that is not easy to stage, and one that will never be replicated; it is a blend of music, poetry, singing, characters, so perfect and so complete, that it leaves nothing to be desired; the girls who interpret kings and other persons are made for their roles . . . there is nothing more sorrowful than to see such an admirable play come to an end; everything

8. Paul Scott links the genre's resurgence to the Fronde. See "The Martyr-Figure as Transgressor in Seventeenth-Century French Theatre" in *Les Lieux Interdits: Transgressions and French Literature*, ed. L. Duffy (Tudor Hull: Hull University Press, 1998), 64.

9. François Hédelin, abbé D'Aubignac, for instance, condemns religious drama in the preface to *Macarise*. See "Observations nécessaires pour l'intelligence de cette allégorie" (Geneva: Slatkine Reprints, 1979), 141.

10. Madame de Sévigné, *Lettres de Madame de Sévigné: de sa famille et de ses amis* (Paris: Hachette, 1863), vol. 6, 283. On La Champmeslé, see Virginia Scott, *Women on the Stage in Early Modern France: 1540–1750* (New York: Cambridge University Press, 2010), 182.

is so simple, so innocent, everything is so sublime and touching . . .
The king approached our seats, and after turning, he addressed me
and said: "Madame, I trust that you enjoyed it." Without being flus-
tered, I responded: "Sire, I am charmed; what I have seen is beyond
words" . . . And then his Majesty took his leave, having made me the
object of envy.[11]

The play became an object of discussion at court and everyone was
pressed to attend. *Esther* was performed at Saint-Cyr six times during
the winter of 1689 and another seven times during that of 1690.

While the biblical references to Esther's attractiveness were down-
played, Racine's play emphasizes the powers of female seductive
charm. In act 1, Esther tells her confidant Elise about how she and her
adoptive father Mardochée uncovered a plot to have the king assas-
sinated. However, unaware of Esther's origins, the king heeds the bad
counsel of Aman, and makes a proclamation to have all of the Jews
in the Persian kingdom exterminated. We learn in act 2 that Aman
is only seeking revenge against Mardochée, who refuses to bow down
to him. In act 3, Esther holds a feast for the king to whom she reveals
her Jewish identity, and accuses Aman of persecuting her people to
satisfy a personal vendetta. In response, the king, whose attraction to
Esther and determination to please her are explicitly stated, allows
Mardochée to take Aman's position and condemns Aman to death.
Afterwards, the Jews are finally liberated.

Although *Esther* received praise, some of Racine's rivals and even
members of the court compared Maintenon to Esther, Queen of the
Jews, and King Louis XIV to King Ahasuerus. But the most scandalous
allusion was the comparison of the king's harem, or the daughters of
Sion, to the Saint-Cyriennes. The passage in act 1 of the play makes
this interpretation entirely credible:

ESTHER. Cependant mon amour pour notre nation
          A rempli ce palais de filles de Sion,
          Jeunes et tendres fleurs par le sort agitées,
          Sous un ciel étranger comme moi transplantées.
          Dans un lieu séparé de profanes témoins,
          Je mets à les former mon étude et mes soins;
          Et c'est là que fuyant l'orgueil du diadème,
          Lasse de vains honneurs, et me cherchant moi-même,

11. Madame de Sévigné, *Lettres* (Paris: Garnier-Flammarion, 1976), 361.

Aux pieds de l'Eternel je viens m'humilier,
Et goûter le plaisir de me faire oublier.

ESTHER. My love for our nation, however,
      Has filled this palace with the daughters of Sion,
      Young and tender flowers, made vulnerable by their plight,
      Living under a foreign sky like myself.
      In a place set apart from irreverent observers,
      I set out to give them my knowledge and my care.
      And fleeing the glory of the crown,
      Weary of vain honors, I find myself,
      At the feet of the Eternal where I come to bow,
      And to taste the pleasure of selflessness.[12]

Several well-documented incidents testify to the effects that the youthful, attractive female performers had on the male members of their audience. Some young men, charmed by the young Saint-Cyriennes, attempted to engage them in amorous intrigues, and a few succeeded.[13] Yet, for Maintenon, the most dangerous outcome of the performance was the effect that flattery had on the female pupils. In a letter written in September 1691, Maintenon expressed her regret at having cultivated such haughtiness:

> I wanted the girls to be witty, to fill their hearts with joy, and to develop their intellect; I have succeeded in this goal: they have wit, and they use it against us; they are puffed up, and more prideful and haughty than even the most powerful princesses ought to be; even according to society, we have formed their intellect, and made them into presumptuous, precocious, and brazen chatterboxes. This is what one accomplishes when one is motivated by a desire to excel.[14]

The spirit of arrogance that dominated the Saint-Cyriennes following the performance of *Esther* was a consequence that Maintenon had neither intended nor desired.

By the end of 1690, Racine had, at Maintenon's request, already finished composing *Athalie*, a play that should have marked the highpoint of the playwright's career, but Maintenon could no longer

12. Racine, *Théâtre Complet*, ed. Alain Viala and Sylvaine Guyot (Paris: Classiques Garnier, 2013), 928.
13. Cambier, *Racine et Madame de Maintenon*, 148.
14. Madame de Maintenon, *Lettres sur l'éducation des filles par Madame de Maintenon*, ed. Théophile Lavallée (Paris: Charpentier, 1854), 77–79.

ignore the backlash from the religious community. Since the very first performance of *Esther*, critics had expressed their hostility toward such an extravagant theatrical representation. The parish priest of Versailles, François Hébert, had always been opposed to the idea of young girls performing in a religious school setting: "This entertainment . . . should be banned from all education . . . All of the convents have their eyes on Saint-Cyr; they will follow your example . . . and, instead of producing novices, they will produce actresses."[15] Others told Maintenon that it was shameful to compromise the young girls who had come to Saint-Cyr for a Christian education by placing them in the public eye.[16] As a result, *Athalie* was performed for a private audience with no costumes or stage scenery. *Athalie* marked not only the end of a playwright's theatrical career but also the end of an era at Saint-Cyr. In a letter dated February 8, 1690, Des Marais, Maintenon's spiritual mentor, had advised Maintenon to find sanctification by reforming Saint-Cyr, and had suggested that she transform Saint-Cyr into a convent.[17] Although Louis XIV had expressed his opposition to this change, Des Marais finally convinced the royal couple, and Saint-Cyr was duly converted on December 1, 1692.

THE DRAMATIC CURRICULUM AFTER *ESTHER*

In response to the *Esther* scandal, Maintenon began to rethink how drama could continue to be implemented at the school. One of the major differences in Saint-Cyr's new theatrical curriculum was the fact that plays were no longer performed in front of an audience. In a letter written February 24, 1701, Maintenon instructed Mme. du Pérou to close theatrical dramatizations to the (male) public:

> You must limit them [dramatic performances] to the classroom, and never let them be seen by outside spectators, under any circumstance. It is always dangerous to allow men to gaze upon attractive young women, who become even more so when they play their roles so well. I tell you, do not admit any man, whether he be poor or rich, young or old, priestly or worldly; or even a saint I say, should he exist in the world. The only thing that we could do if a superior wanted to see,

15. Émile Faguet, *Madame de Maintenon Institutrice* (Paris: Oudin, 1885), xvii.
16. Caylus, *Souvenirs*, 97.
17. Maintenon, *Correspondance Générale de Madame de Maintenon*, ed. Théophile Lavallée (Paris: Charpentier, 1865–66), 3: 219.

indeed, just what these plays are like, would be to perform the short ones, as we have done.[18]

Although other authors continued to compose religious plays for the Saint-Cyriennes,[19] it was the short secular conversations and proverbs that played a primary role in the reform of the theatrical curriculum at Saint-Cyr. Maintenon's improvisational dramatic proverbs were inspired by those favored in courtly society toward the end of the seventeenth century. Each plot illustrated a well-known adage that was not stated in the text itself, so that as in traditional salon games, the pupils were invited to decipher its message, which would in turn lead to a discussion. Maintenon's conversations, or dialogues, allowed each female pupil to speak in turn and to give her point of view on various moral values or specific vices. While these short secular dramatic genres were originally created in the salons, Maintenon gave them a pedagogical purpose. Indeed, Marie-Emmanuelle Plagnol-Diéval credits Maintenon with having conceived of pedagogical genres that would be further developed by such writers as Mme. de Genlis and Mme. Campan in the eighteenth century.[20]

The conversations and proverbs emphasized three major lessons that sought to make amends for the damage done to the minds of the Saint-Cyriennes during the season of *Esther*: that courtly society and its favorite pastimes, such as theater, were to be avoided (or, rather, adapted); that young women must safeguard their reputations; and that one should take pleasure in one's domestic work and daily routines. Furthermore, if the Saint-Cyriennes had previously dreamed of fairytale weddings, the conversations and proverbs convinced them of the stark realities of conjugal life. While *Esther* had provided the Saint-Cyriennes with an opportunity to engage with courtly society, the conversations and proverbs conditioned the Saint-Cyriennes to reject courtly society and to be aware of its false luster.

18. Maintenon, *Lettres sur l'éducation des filles*, 215–216.

19. For instance, see two plays by De Boyer: *Jephté*, performed in 1692 at Saint-Cyr, and *Judith*, written for Saint-Cyr, but staged at the Comédie Française in 1695. See Henry Carrington Lancaster, *A History of French Dramatic Literature* (Baltimore: The Johns Hopkins Press, 1929; New York: Gordonian Press, 1966), vol. 4, 292–332. See also Perry Gethner's article in the present volume.

20. Marie-Emmanuelle Plagnol-Diéval, *Madame de Genlis et le théâtre d'éducation au XVIIIe siècle* (Oxford: Voltaire Foundation, 1997).

As the performance of *Esther* had demonstrated, association with courtly society quickly led to scandal. Thus, the proverb "One fish caught is worth the fisher's effort" (*"Toujours pêche qui en prend un"*) warns women against courtly society and its allure. In the proverb, Mme. Duceaux, a woman of independent means who does not squander her wealth or compromise her reputation, finds peace and contentment by living away from court. She serves as an example to young girls and employs logical arguments to discourage them from excess. Mme. Duceaux tells Mlle. Dubreuil that her consistent pleasure-seeking will eventually leave her feeling empty: "Haven't you seen yourself that amusement never conforms to our expectations of it, and that one is hardly ever satisfied on the days that one sets aside for recreational activities?"[21] For Mlle. Denneville, who is obsessed with the idea of living at court, Mme. Duceaux offers an image of courtly life resembling a tragic play in which one must constantly wear a mask:

> One always needs to dissimulate, to appear sad if the king is, even when one is not; to express joy if it's expected, although one is full of sorrow; to be consistently bored, because one never does what one wants; to speak contrary to one's opinion, to conform to theirs, to indulge all of their passions; to sacrifice sleep, health, and often one's conscience.[22]

Mme. Duceaux possesses a spiritual quality of self-sacrifice that makes it clear that she is Maintenon's mouthpiece. She alludes to the theological concept of the eternal discontentment of the human heart. Pleasure and desire can never be quenched because only God can fill our hearts.

In the conversation "On Glory" (*"Sur la bonne gloire"*), a woman's glory is directly associated with her reputation. "Glory" is defined as "incapable of baseness" and entirely blameless.[23] As John J. Conley notes, this definition of glory is placed "within a gendered framework" and a good reputation is a noblewoman's "most impor-

21. All quotations from the conversations are drawn from *Les loisirs de Madame de Maintenon*, ed. Constant Venesoen (Paris: Classiques Garnier, 2011). Those from the proverbs are drawn from *Proverbes inédits*, ed. M. de Monmerqué (Paris: Imprimerie de E. Pochard, 1829). *Proverbes inédits*, 279.
22. *Proverbes inédits*, 286–87.
23. *Les loisirs de Madame de Maintenon*, 98.

tant personal possession."[24] Thus, it highlights a double standard for women. The speakers in this conversation maintain that a woman must "prefer boredom to amusement for fear of compromising her reputation."[25] Throughout the conversations, it is clearly noted that frequent participation in any favorite pastimes, such as going to the theater, will tarnish a young woman's reputation. The more a woman places herself on public display, the more her good character will be called into question by courtly society.

The proverb "The pitcher that often goes to the well will break in the end" ("*Tant va la cruche à l'eau qu'à la fin elle se brise*") is an illustration of the importance of carefully guarding one's reputation. Céline spends her days preparing for balls and other diversions that she attends with a certain *mondaine* by the name of Mme. de Saint-Fargeot. A friend of her mother, Mme. d'Arlincour, warns Céline about her inevitable fall from grace: "It is the pursuit of pleasure that destroys persons of our sex, and, when a woman is not content with distractions she finds in her own home, her reputation is soon compromised."[26] Mme. d'Arlincour is well aware of the fact that women are judged more harshly than men, owing to the emphasis placed on a woman's chastity. Mme. d'Arlincour, having remained at home during her youth, was rewarded with a husband who allowed her to have absolute authority in the home. The proverb therefore emphasizes the power that virtuous women may exercise in the family by maintaining their reputation. Throughout the pedagogical plays, Maintenon attempted to shape the Saint-Cyriennes' attitudes toward remaining at home and avoiding courtly society during their youth, by making them believe that they would in turn have more power and influence when they were married.

To dissuade the Saint-Cyriennes from seeking lives as socialites, the proverbs and conversations encouraged them to find joy in simple domestic tasks. In the proverb "Whoever counts without his host counts twice" ("*Qui compte sans son hôte compte deux fois*") Mlles. Alexandrine and Clotilde disagree with Mlle. Mélanie, reminding her that the kind of woman who goes to the theater jeopardizes her

---

24. John J. Conley, *The Suspicion of Virtue: Women Philosophers in Neoclassical France* (Ithaca and London: Cornell University Press, 2002), 147.

25. *Les loisirs de Madame de Maintenon*, 99.

26. Ibid., 124–25.

reputation by making too many public appearances.[27] Mlle. Alexandrine depicts the ideal *honnête femme* as one who protects her reputation by remaining engaged in domestic activities:

> An *honnête femme* gets up in the morning to have more time, she begins with a prayer, she gives orders to her servants, she sees her children, she tends to their instruction, she takes care to receive those whom her husband sometimes invites to dinner, who are not always to her liking; she is the first servant in her home to make preparations; after the meal she stays with the company in spite of herself and when she is finally left alone, she works on her needlework or her own affairs, she writes to lenders, she rarely goes out: the day finally comes to an end, she begins again the next day.[28]

The *honnête femme* thus rejects a social life and chooses to remain at home. Mlle. Alexandrine even goes as far to claim that this woman is happy, peaceful, and wealthy, and does not feel the need to go out in public.

The emphasis placed on such concepts as tranquility, solitude, rest, and work promoted values that did not enter easily into the minds of young women who aspired to having lives defined by a full social calendar. It was counterintuitive for them, as noblewomen, to resign themselves to a life that esteemed domesticity and discouraged the pursuit of pleasure. For instance, the conversation *On work* (*Sur le travail*) advances the idea that one must find pleasure in one's domestic work. Mlle. Odile who feels "deprived of the pleasure of recreation and promenade" wonders "what pleasure can be taken by working."[29] Mlle. Clémentine affirms that if a young woman becomes accustomed to domestic work, she will be above all reproach. Mlle. Hortense states that work is in itself pleasurable since it calms the passions, occupies the mind, and banishes laziness, which is the mother of all vices. Further, she states that it is especially disadvantageous if a member of their sex can neither "remain at home, nor find pleasure in housework" since she will seek diversion in "gambling, society, and theater."[30] She notes that there can be nothing more damaging to a young woman's reputation and to her piety than to be seen engaging in such public events. To Mlle. Odile, who demon-

---

27. *Proverbes inédits*, 189.
28. Ibid., 190.
29. *Les loisirs de Madame de Maintenon*, 214
30. Ibid., 216–17.

strates her distaste of domestic work, Mlle. Hortense retorts "it is in bad taste to live at the expense of one's family without contributing anything in return."[31] Mlle. Hortense responds to the reality of the economic crisis facing the aristocracy at the end of the seventeenth century. Women of status could no longer afford to devote their time and energy to social engagement and were encouraged to engage in "work" at home.

Although the conversations and proverbs place the emphasis on domestic tasks, conjugal life is not depicted in a positive light. For instance, in the conversation *On constraint in all conditions* (*Sur la contrainte de tous les États*), the most experienced woman describes the typical husband as unpredictable and given to tyrannical behavior toward his spouse: "You may displease him [your husband], maybe he will displease you: it is almost impossible to like the same things; he may have a tendency to overspend: he might be stingy, and deny you everything. It would disturb you, if I told you what marriage is like."[32] Furthermore, in the conversation *On the inconvenience of marriage* (*Sur les inconvéniens du mariage*), Mlle. Alexandrine equates marriage with slavery: "A woman must sacrifice herself to death and slavery by marrying, and there are but many examples."[33] Although the proverbs express a negative view of marriage, they laud the satisfaction to be gained by embracing a rigorous daily routine.

In sum, Maintenon's proverbs and conversations, intended to entertain, nevertheless carried a very serious warning concerning courtly society and its *divertissements* (diversions). After the *Esther* debacle, Maintenon attempted to wean the Saint-Cyriennes off their obsession with courtly society. In her pedagogical "plays," Maintenon attempted to entice the Saint-Cyriennes into isolation by demonstrating how a conservative lifestyle as a young single woman would lead to more empowerment in the home as a married woman. Yet, given the mixed message concerning conjugal life, it is not surprising that the Saint-Cyriennes opted to join convents.

For Maintenon, the theater in itself was not an enemy of morality. She had made every effort to include performing arts in the curriculum at Saint-Cyr from the very beginning of its establishment. As an educator, Maintenon valued the theater's dual capacities to instruct

31. Ibid., 218.
32. Ibid., 210–211.
33. Ibid., 191.

as well as entertain. Yet, the disastrous effects that *Esther* had had on the Saint-Cyriennes demonstrated the potential threat it posed to the lives of women, whose future depended so much on their virtue remaining intact. Maintenon was forced to realize that women in the theater, whether on- or offstage, placed themselves in the public eye. The more a woman appeared in public, the more she risked its judgment and becoming the object of its desire, as in the case of the actresses in *Esther*. Thus, the proverbs and conversations that Maintenon wrote were an attempt to maintain a theatrical curriculum at Saint-Cyr while shielding the Saint-Cyriennes from the public eye. (Ironically, Maintenon employed the same dramatic games she had played in the salons to warn young women against the dangers of courtly society and its excessive *divertissements*.) At the same time these proverbs and conversations led the Saint-Cyriennes away from the idea that once they left Saint-Cyr, they would embrace all of the freedoms to which they aspired as noblewomen. The conversations and proverbs attempted to "seduce" them instead into thinking they would find more pleasure in domestic work, and would thus enjoy more agency within the domestic sphere. In this way, Maintenon was trying to reinforce the school's mission to produce virtuous wives and mothers to repopulate a crumbling elite class.

Yet because the proverbs and conversations systematically depicted domestic and conjugal life in a rigorous way, Maintenon's efforts did not convince the Saint-Cyriennes to commit to such an existence. The concepts of hard work, modesty, and self-restraint were difficult to instill in young noblewomen who believed that their titles would give them all that life had to offer. Clearly, between domestic life and convent life, they found convent life to be the lesser of two evils. Perhaps the *Esther* debacle set women back in more ways than we realize.

CHRISTOPHER SEMK

Bossuet's Ticklish Subjects: Preaching and Pleasure

We do not usually think of sermons as entertaining. Intended to edify and evangelize, the sermon is an instance of pastoral theology and any pleasure derived from it must accordingly be secondary to its theological purpose. At the same time, the sermon is a kind of oratory and thus borrows from the toolbox of other forms of public speaking. Consequently, a sermon's theatricality as well as its "literariness" —its structure, style, use of metaphor and other rhetorical figures— invites an appreciation of its aesthetic qualities. In seventeenth-century France, sermons, especially those given by famous preachers on saints' feast days or during the Advent and Lenten seasons, were as eagerly anticipated as any pop star's concert is today.[1] The time and place of the sermon would be advertised in advance, wealthy attendees would send their servants ahead of them to secure good seats, and afterward the laity would evaluate the sermon's rhetorical merits in addition to, and sometimes apart from, its doctrinal message. For concerned preachers, such misplaced enthusiasm for the sermon's aesthetic value perversely twisted its instructive purpose into mere entertainment. In the words of Jacques-Bénigne Bossuet (1627–1704), when the public seeks only pleasure from sermons, priests become "ministers of pleasure" and the sermon "an enjoyable talk that merely tickles the ears."[2]

---

1. Madame de Sévigné's enthusiasm for Bourdaloue is emblematic in this regard. See Sévigné to Madame de Grignan, March 13, 1671, in *Lettres*, ed. Bernard Raffalli (Paris: Garnier-Flammarion, 1976), 83–85.

2. Jacques-Béninge Bossuet, "Sermon sur la parole de Dieu" and "Sermon sur la prédication évangélique," in *Sermons*, ed. Constance Cagnat-Debœuf (Paris: Folio, 2001), 86. Unless indicated otherwise, all translations are by the author.

YFS 130, *Guilty Pleasures: Theater, Piety, and Immorality in Seventeenth-Century France*, ed. Harris and Prest, © 2016 by Yale University.

The "tickled" or ticklish ears that Bossuet evokes are, on the one hand, a homiletic commonplace originating in Paul's epistles and mobilized by generations of preachers who condemned their audience's aversion to unpleasant doctrinal truths in favor of sermons that pandered to their own desires or accommodated their secular lifestyle. On the other hand, this auricular tickle ties the experience of pleasure to the sense of touch, and the sense of touch to that of hearing. As such, it is not simply a question of a listener's desire to hear doctrine that confirms and comforts his or her own beliefs, but rather an automatic physiological response. In this curious commingling of audition and tactility, the threat of "tickling the ears" and consequently of the sermon's aestheticization seem to inhabit nearly every instance of public preaching.

The seventeenth century—arguably the golden age of both theater and anti-theatrical sentiment in France—was a period during which vision played a central role not only in the dramatic arts, but also in epistemology. As a result, scholars have largely come to regard the seventeenth century as the period during which the "modern" subject was born—a subject that is autonomous, disembodied, and above all, visual in its relationship to the world.[3] Such emphasis on sight leads to the exclusion or at least to the marginalization of the other members of the early modern sensorium: hearing, touch, taste, and smell. However, recent scholarship has shed light on the roles that the other senses played in the culture and epistemology of the seventeenth century, allowing us to grasp a more richly textured model of the early modern subject.[4] In this essay, I would like to investigate the theatricality of the early modern sermon through a paradigm of sound rather than sight. Here, I suggest that for Bossuet the homiletic commonplace of "ticklish ears" describes the pleasures of hearing as a consequence of both his "incarnate poetics," according to which language is understood as corporeal, and his adoption of a physiological

---

3. Martin Jay, in *Downcast Eyes: The Denigration of Vision in Twentieth-Century French Thought* (Berkeley and Los Angeles: University of California Press, 1994), identifies the Cartesian "valorization of the disembodied eye" with the observational and perspectival practices of modern science and art (81).

4. See especially Erec Koch's *The Aesthetic Body* (Newark: University of Delaware Press, 2008). For a general reconsideration of the passions, see *Reading the Early Modern Passions*, ed. Gail Kern Paster, Katherine Rowe, and Mary Floyd-Wilson (Philadelphia: University of Pennsylvania Press, 2004).

model of pleasure as *chatouillement*, or a tickling sensation.[5] The human ear, as we shall see, is for Bossuet the primary organ through which Christian doctrine reaches the soul. Yet the human ear is also an ear of flesh and, as such, the sense of hearing is corrupt. Without the corrective of a metaphorical "inner" ear that listens carefully to the doctrine enveloped in the preacher's voice, the ear is just as likely—if not more likely—to be tickled by the rhythm, tone, accent, and other modalities of the sermon's oral delivery.

When discussing the theatricality of the sermon, we often refer to its appeal to the visual through the trope of hypotyposis—the power of words to stimulate the imagination and "set before the eyes" people, places, and things that are both spatially and temporally removed from the moment of enunciation. The famous opening of Bossuet's *Sermon sur la mort* (Sermon on Death) (1662), for example, promises to open up a tomb before the "delicate eyes" of his aristocratic audience. This visual dimension of the early modern sermon suggests affinities with the stage, the absolute counter-model of the pulpit. In the *Sermon sur la parole de Dieu* (Sermon on the Word of God) (1661), Bossuet notes that the fourth-century Church Father John Chrysostom, whose treatise *On the Priesthood* represents one of the first sustained reflections on homiletic theory and practice, often reproached his congregation for listening to his sermons as though they were at the theater. Preaching, Chrysostom writes, is difficult because the public, accustomed to theatrical entertainment, more closely resembles a crowd of spectators (*theatis*) than disciples.[6] Bossuet explicates Chrysostom's remarks in terms that announce his *Maximes et réflexions sur la comédie* (1694): "These animated representations . . . are dangerous insofar as they do not delight unless they move, unless they interest the spectator, unless they make him perform his role as well, without being part of the play and without getting on stage."[7] The spectacle invites the spectator to identify with the characters, to share in their love, their ambition, and their suffering, and thus to be transformed (harmfully) by the performance. When reading Bossuet's anti-theatrical remarks, we take for granted that the eye is the

---

5. I borrow the expression "incarnate poetics" from Thérèse Goyet, *L'humanisme de Bossuet*, I (Paris: Klincksieck, 1965), 681.

6. Chrysostom, *Peri hierosynes* V.1.11–36.

7. Bossuet, *Sermons*, 311.

organ through which the spectacle takes hold. In their disapproval of the stage, seventeenth-century anti-theatrical writers such as Pierre Nicole (1625–1695) and Bernard Lamy (1640–1715) focused on the theater's appeal to idolatrous eyes. Nicole advocated turning away from theatrical entertainments and, indeed, from the dangers of society more generally, in favor of silent self-examination and reflection. Turning the outward gaze inward, this voluntary "salvific blindness" closes the spectator's idolatrous eyes to the enthralling visions of the stage and thereby preserves the integrity of the soul.[8]

But what of the ears, which cannot be so easily or so fully closed? And what of the pleasures of listening to a sermon with the same "idolatrous ears" with which one listens to a play?[9] After all, attending the theater is as much an aural experience as a visual one. In a well-known passage in the *Confessions*, Augustine recounts how his friend Alypius agreed to attend a gladiatorial spectacle with his eyes firmly shut, believing this would protect him from the dangers of spectatorship. Alypius's eyelids proved, however, to be a meager defense against the spectacle's charms, for Alypius was so overwhelmed by the applause, the cries, and the clamor of the arena that he opened his eyes and instantly fell victim to the allure of the spectacle. Augustine's anecdote highlights the vulnerability of the ears, which are not only always open, but also expose the subject to attack from either side, rendering him or her defenseless.[10] So the ear may be just as, if not more, susceptible than the eye to the pleasures of the stage.

In addition, if we consider the theater as the counter-model of the pulpit in homiletic literature, it cannot be by virtue of vision or spectacle alone, for homiletics is above all the oral transmission and audible reception of Christian doctrine. Indeed, Bossuet's reflection on the theater cited above makes no mention of vision. Moreover, this remark appears in the context of a sermon on the reception of the Word of God, not in an anti-theatrical tract. If Chrysostom's congregants listened to his sermon as though they were at the theater, Bossuet argues, it is because their enthusiasm, their tears, and their applause (applause during sermons was not uncommon in

8. See Laurent Thirouin's excellent book on the subject, *L'aveuglement salutaire: Le réquisitoire contre le théâtre dans la France classique* (Paris: Honoré Champion, 2007).

9. The expression belongs to Rotrou; see his *Le véritable Saint Genest* (1647), 1.5.

10. For more on the vulnerability of the ear, see Denis Guénoun, "L'oreille seule," in *L'exhibition des mots* (Paris: Circé, 1998), 44–58.

Chrysostom's time) were superficial "theatrical affections animated by springs and artifice."[11] Moved by the acoustic qualities of the preacher's words, the audience nevertheless fails to understand the message contained therein. Thus the theatricality of the sermon may reside elsewhere than in the visual tropes that a preacher deploys or the superficial resemblance of the pulpit to the stage. It may be the preacher's voice, and the effects it produces on the listener, that render the sermon theatrical.

In spite of the longstanding traditional hierarchy of the senses that places sight at the pinnacle, hearing emerges in spiritual writing as the crucial sense, even more important than sight, for accessing religious truth. The dynamic scene of enfleshment that opens the Gospel of John heralds the arrival of a divinity that is the *Word* incarnate, and whose message is articulated by human voices; through the Incarnation, the divine is audible as well as visible. In spiritual practice, hearing is important for both public worship and private devotion, in singing, chanting, praying, and of course, preaching. "Faith comes through hearing," wrote Paul in Romans 10:7, paving the way for generations of sacred orators. In the early seventeenth century, the theologian Pierre Charron (1541–1603) placed the ear above the eye in the hierarchy of the senses, recalling the Pauline claim that "Christianity teaches that faith and salvation come through hearing."[12] The ear's receptivity to spiritual truths was not without pitfalls, however, as Charron reminds his readers that it is also through the ear that one may be turned toward good or evil.

For Bossuet, too, hearing is the sense necessary for faith. In a sermon preached on the second Sunday of Lent in 1660, he argues before his "Christian audience" that the "renewed" human being, living after Christ's mortal sojourn, "has only the sense of hearing."[13] While this link between hearing and faith is obvious in homiletics, Bossuet further illustrates his point by describing the most visual (and theatrical) of the sacraments—the Eucharist—as a wholly aural affair: "In this adorable sacrament all of your senses trick you, except the sense of hearing."[14] In this remarkable passage that recalls René Descartes' description of melted wax (but toward a very different end), Bossuet

11. Bossuet, *Sermons*, 311.
12. Pierre Charron, *De la sagesse* (Bordeaux: Simon Millanges, 1601), 107–8.
13. Bossuet, *Œuvres* IX, 93.
14. Bossuet, ibid.

describes how the communicant sees a small round wafer and tastes the dryness of the bread, yet hears the priest intone the transformative words *Hoc est enim corpus meum* ("This is my body").

For Bossuet, then, as for Paul, the ear is without a doubt the organ of faith. Yet the understanding of its operation—how it transmits sound to the cognitive faculty—underwent a major transformation in the seventeenth century. In his study of the "aesthetic body," Erec Koch traces a shift in the conception of voice from the representation of an affect, to be grasped intellectually, toward a force that elicits an affective response.[15] In other words, the seventeenth century witnessed a change in emphasis from the production of sound by the vocal organs to its reception by the ear. Koch convincingly argues that this move from voice as representation toward voice as force may be attributed to the rise of a mechanistic understanding of the human body according to which audition depends upon forces or vibrations acting upon the organs of the ear. Drawing parallels between treatises on rhetoric and physiologies of hearing, Koch highlights how "language vehiculated passion by vocal sound in the modalities of tone, accent, and inflexion," what linguists call the prosodic features of spoken language.[16] Similarly, musicologist Veit Erlmann has recently investigated the affective response elicited by sound in the early modern subject, arguing that "sympathetic resonance"—the phenomenon by which a body (e.g. a string or the organs of the ear) responds to vibrations in the air—implied the dissolution of boundaries between the hearer and what is heard and thus challenged the integrity of an autonomous, reasoning subject.[17] This physiological understanding of audition as the result of vibrations in the organs of the ear sustains Bossuet's reflections on preaching and pleasure.[18] The "tickled" ears of his listeners ultimately highlight the corruption of the senses as a consequence of embodiment.

The relationship between "ticklish ears" and embodiment reflects, negatively, the relationship between the preacher's voice and the In-

15. Erec Koch, *The Aesthetic Body*, 140–41.

16. Ibid.,176.

17. Veit Erlmann, *Reason and Resonance: A History of Modern Aurality* (Brooklyn: Zone Books, 2010), 29–68.

18. Bossuet may have received firsthand knowledge of the structures of the ear while attending the anatomist Duverney's lessons at Versailles. See Fontenelle's "Éloge de Duverney," *Œuvres complètes VII*, ed. Alain Niderst (Paris: Fayard, 1994), 189–98. See also Alain Bouchet, "Bossuet: Adepte méconnu de Descartes en anatomie et physiologie," *Histoire des sciences médicales* 3 (1999): 255–66.

carnation. What we know of Bossuet's thought on the art of preaching may be gleaned only from his sermons, since he wrote no treatise on homiletics or manual for young preachers, aside from a short instructional text on the style of the Church Fathers.[19] There is a remarkable theological coherence in Bossuet's view of the preacher's task in his sermons: the doctrine of the Incarnation, the Word made flesh, plays a fundamental role, so much so that for Bossuet preaching is analogous to the sacrament of the Eucharist. The *Sermon sur la parole de Dieu*, the *Sermon sur la prédication évangélique* (Sermon on Preaching the Gospel) (1662), and the *Panégyrique de l'Apôtre Saint Paul* (In Praise of St. Paul the Apostle) (1657), and the two earlier *Panégyriques de Saint Gorgon* (In Priase of Saint Gorgon) (1649, 1654) all demonstrate that the link between the altar and the pulpit, the Eucharistic wafer and the preacher's voice, had occupied Bossuet from his earliest days at the pulpit. This sacramental link between word and wafer has several consequences. First, it would seem that for a lifelong adversary of the Protestants such as Bossuet, yoking the altar to the pulpit confers upon sacred oratory a central place in Catholic worship. Bossuet also uses the altar to authorize the pulpit, which commands as much respect and attention from the faithful as the sacrament of the Eucharist does. For Bossuet, the priesthood consists in the ministry of the Word as much as it does the ministry of the Eucharist.

Bossuet illustrates the link between the evangelical word and the Eucharistic wafer through a quotation from the third-century theologian Origen, who described the Gospel as a kind of "second body" of Christ.[20] Bossuet explicates Origen's comment by arguing that God twice made himself perceptible to the human senses: first, through the mystery of the Incarnation and, second, through the ministry of the Word. In the *Sermon sur la Parole de Dieu*, Bossuet reprises this passage from Origen and explicitly joins hearing to the doctrine of the Incarnation. Significantly, immediately before the *Ave* that traditionally followed the sermon's exordium, Bossuet reminds his audience that it was through the sense of hearing that Christ was conceived in Mary's womb: "Come and learn . . . the word of the very Son of God, through the prayers of she who conceived him, first, says St.

19. Bossuet, "Sur le style des Pères de l'Eglise," *Littératures classiques* 46 (2002): 221–29.

20. "Panis iste, quem deus verbum corpus suum esse fatetur; verbum est nutritorium animarum." Origen, *Commentary on Matthew 85*. Quoted in the *Panégyrique de l'apôtre saint Paul*, 392.

Augustine, through the ear, and who . . . made herself worthy of conceiving Him in her blessed womb."[21] This passage alludes to the patristic metaphor, falsely attributed to Augustine, according to which the Virgin was impregnated through the ear (*et virgo per aurem impregnabatur*). This developed into a popular belief, satirized by Molière, that Mary conceived Christ through the ear, thereby maintaining her virginity.[22] For Bossuet, the ear is the organ through which faith takes root and through which the Word becomes flesh. The surest sign that the Word has taken root in fertile ground lies in the behavior of the congregants who take to heart the lessons of the sermon and adjust their lives accordingly. Otherwise, their tears, sighs, nods of approval, and enthusiastic acclaim are nothing but "theatrical affections, animated by springs and artifice."[23] The incarnate word, with its tone, rhythm, and inflexion, is thus capable of stirring the passions of the audience without bringing about any true conversion.

The attentive listener must train his or her ear not to the rhythm and intonation of the human voice, but rather to the doctrinal truth contained in the sermon. This does not mean, however, that audible words are unnecessary or superfluous. The Word, understood as participating in the mystery of the Incarnation, is in fact dignified by its corporeality: "Do not think," Bossuet admonishes his audience, "that you ought to look down on this sensual and exterior word."[24] Indeed, as Bossuet's fellow bishop and sometime theological sparring partner Fénelon remarked, human beings, as embodied creatures, are unable to grasp abstract spiritual lessons by intellect alone. Fénelon writes: "Man is entirely engulfed in sensual things," and consequently, "it is necessary to give a body to all the instruction that we wish to impart."[25] For Bossuet too, Christian mysteries must first be apprehended by the senses. This is a direct consequence of the Incarnation, through which an invisible deity appears in a sensual form, first in a human body and by extension in the sacrament of the Eucharist. Preaching, as an office analogous to the celebration of the Eucharist,

21. *Œuvres*, 115.

22. The phrase is well attested in devotional literature. In *L'école des femmes* (1662), Molière exploits the comedic potential of the *conceptio per aurem*: "Elle . . . me vint demander / Avec une innocence à nulle autre pareille, / Si les enfants qu'on fait se faisaient par l'oreille." (1.1.162–4). (She . . . came to ask me, in complete innocence, if babies were made through the ear.)

23. *Sermons*, 311.

24. *Œuvres*, 126.

25. Fénelon, *Œuvres complètes* VII (Paris: Briand, 1810), 52.

similarly entails a kind of incarnation by enclosing the Word in an audible envelope.[26] While this "incarnate poetics" germane to preaching promises to deploy the gamut of rhetorical inventions for theological purposes, it also raises the possibility of taking pleasure in the
sermon's structure, its literary qualities, and the preacher's voice. In
other words, it may "tickle" the ears rather than penetrate the heart.

The tickle that results in physical pleasure rather than moral
profit had, by Bossuet's time, become something of a homiletic commonplace. The trope of ticklish ears can be traced back to the New
Testament. In 2 Timothy 4:3–4, Paul writes disapprovingly of congregants who have "itching" or "ticklish" ears. Such men and women
prefer listening to religious teachers who flatter their own desires
and interests—thereby relieving the "itch"—than those who preach
sound doctrine, which is often unpleasant to hear and aims to convert
rather than to please. "After their own lusts," Paul writes, "shall they
heap to themselves teachers, having itching ears."[27] The Biblical turn
of phrase entered into both English ("to have itching ears" and "to
tickle the ears") and French (*chatouiller les oreilles*) as a fixed expression that in both languages today means simply "to flatter." This is
of course the sense in which Paul originally employed the term. The
auricular "itch" has a rich semantic history, however, and Bossuet's
censure of sermons that "tickle the ears" reflects a uniquely early
modern and mechanistic understanding of tickling as synonymous
with physical pleasure.

In homiletic literature, "ticklish" generally describes the attitude
of the improper listener, who attends to the texture of the voice, the
preacher's deployment of rhetorical figures, and what we might call
the literary or aesthetic merits of the sermon. The figure of the improper listener haunts early modern reflections on preaching. Antoine Godeau (1605–1672), for example, decried those who attended
sermons "to delight in them," thereby transforming the pulpit into
a playhouse.[28] The Jesuit Antoine Sirmond (1591–1643) composed an
entire treatise on preaching and listening, *L'auditeur de la parole de
Dieu* (1638), in which he instructs congregants how best to listen to
the word of God. Listening, as a skill that required concentration and

---

26. *Œuvres*, 126.
27. 2 Timothy 4:3–4. Bossuet elliptically alludes to this passage in the 1663 *Sermon sur la parole de Dieu*.
28. Antoine Godeau, *Discours sur les ordres sacrez* (Paris: Joubert, 1686), 206.

a devout attitude, is a practice distinct from hearing, an automatic physiological operation. The improper listener seeks (or "itches") to be entertained. Paul's expression "itching (*knetho*) ears" derives from the Greek verb *knethein*, "to scrape," implying palpable relief or gratification.[29] Thus "ticklish" here does not describe any physiological quality of the auditory system, but rather the moral disposition of the listener. Paul's condemnation, however, aims at more than one target. Congregants who wish to be entertained seek out teachers who will entertain them; in turn, preachers who are concerned about their reputation among their congregants may be tempted to adjust their teachings accordingly. Worse still, the Vulgate translated Paul's expression as *prurientes auribus*, which carries the added connotation of depravity or lasciviousness. "To have itching ears," then, could also be rendered as "to have prurient ears," translating the desire to hear not just any pleasing or flattering discourse, but rather a titillating tale, juicy bit of gossip, or off-color remark. This is an important nuance, because it emphasizes illicit, erotic, or carnal pleasure—an especially wicked perversion of the sermon's purpose. To be tickled by a sermon, then, translates a moral failure on the part of the ticklish listener.

Yet "ticklish" also describes a physical property intrinsic to human beings. Aristotle, in *On the Parts of Animals*, notes the unparalleled tenderness of human skin, the exquisite delicacy of which explains both the human being's finely tuned sense of touch and the uniquely human capacity to be tickled: "The fact that human beings only are susceptible to tickling is due to the fineness (*aesthetikotaton*) of their skin."[30] Aristotle goes on to associate tickling with laughter (another exclusively human phenomenon), but in early

---

29. Though arguably the most well-known example, Paul's expression is not the only instance of the metaphor of tickled ears in Antiquity. Lucian of Samosata employs a similar expression in his dialogue on dance, *Peri orcheseos*, in which Crato chastises Lycinus for abandoning serious philosophy in order to delight in popular entertainments, thus having his ears "tickled with a feather." Philodemus, in his treatise on music, contends that music, as sound without meaning (and so distinct from language), "tickles" the ears (*Peri mousikes* col. 78.30–31). Similarly, Seneca, in his *Letters to Lucilius* (*Ep.* 108.5), laments that philosophy has become a pastime for crowds who seek frivolous pleasure (*delectandas aures*) rather than moral instruction. All these examples deprecate the pleasure occasioned by tickling, linking it to the meaningless, frivolous, and irrational.

30. Aristotle, *On the Parts of Animals*, trans. A. L. Peck (Cambridge: Harvard University Press, 1961), 281.

modern France tickling became synonymous with physical pleasure. In his *Dictionnaire universel*, Antoine Furetière defines *chatouiller* in the following terms: "to touch lightly someone in a delicate spot, such that it causes pleasure or emotion."[31] He continues, adding that *chatouiller* is also employed to designate the sensation of pleasure. Thus, just as music or an agreeable voice could be said to "tickle" the ears, flavorsome food "tickles" the palate, and pleasing odors "tickle" the nose. For Furetière, like Aristotle, the ticklish sensation, or indeed pleasure, depends on the delicacy of the tickled area. Unlike Aristotle, Furetière extends the ticklish sensation to the full range of human senses. As for Bossuet, the bishop marvels at the delicacy of the inner ear (the tympanic membrane and the malleus) in the *Traité de la connaissance de Dieu et de soi-même* (Treatise on Knowing God and Oneself, published posthumously in 1741) as "this film, extremely thin and taut, that, thanks to a little hammer of extraordinary delicate fabrication, receives the agitation of the air and transmits it to the brain through the nerves."[32] Taking into account the extreme delicacy of the auditory system, it would seem that it is precisely the delicacy of the ear that renders human beings especially susceptible to hearing sermons as pleasurable, to having their ears "tickled."

While we tend to associate tickling with tactile sensations only, during the early modern period tickling could be more broadly applied to any pleasing sensation. It was Descartes who posited tickling as a mechanism for pleasure (and, in excess, pain). In his posthumous *Traité de l'homme* (1664), Descartes defines tickling as a kind of "corporeal pleasure" and thus opposes it, naturally, to "*douleur*," pain.[33] In the *Traité de l'âme* (1649), Descartes explicitly links tickling with pleasure, writing that the sensation arises when the nerves are excited by the sensory input.[34] The difference between tickling and pain is one of degree: if the force acts too strongly upon the nerves, the sensation becomes unbearable and results in pain. Even tickling, itself a pleasurable sensation, can become an agonizing (and allegedly fatal) experience when prolonged. Descartes accounts for the deeply

31. Furetière, *Dictionnaire universel* (The Hague: Leers, 1690), 378.

32. Bossuet, *Traité de la connaissance de Dieu et de soi-même* (Paris: Garnier, 1937), 71.

33. Descartes, "Traité de l'homme," in *Œuvres de Descartes*, ed. Charles Adam and Paul Tannery, XI, 143–44.

34. Descartes, "Traité de l'âme," in *Œuvres de Descartes*, XI, 399.

subjective nature of pain and pleasure by positing that these sensations also depend on the physical constitution and mental disposition of the subject. He illustrates this through an analogy with tragic pleasure, where painful passions such as sadness or hate can induce pleasurable sensations in the spectator. Pleasure arises from the spectator's awareness that the passions, which, in another context, might cause real suffering, are, in the theater, harmless. The dramatic representation of sadness, hate, anger, and other typically painful passions thus appear (*semblent*) to tickle (*chatouiller*) the soul, resulting in pleasure.[35] Presumably, when confronted with real grief, the same spectator would feel pain because the agitation of the nerves would no longer seem to tickle, but actually hurt. Descartes's preference for the term *chatouillement* in the *Traité des passions* and elsewhere may have been strategic: by employing a physical term rather than words more commonly used to designate pleasure (e.g. *volupté*), Descartes situates pleasure squarely within the physiological realm and thus deftly avoids addressing the thorny theological and moral problems associated with the ancient tradition that viewed pleasure as an appetite of the soul. In fact, for Descartes, tickling, and the resulting joy, could even serve as a foundation for ethical behavior.[36] That the sensation that elicits laughter, tears, or both should lie at the root of moral philosophy comes as no surprise when one remembers that, as Aristotle observed, ticklishness is a property unique to human beings.

Bossuet was certainly no stranger to natural and moral philosophy and cautiously embraced the scientific advancements of his day. In his Cartesian *Traité de la connaissance de Dieu et de soi-même*, Bossuet employs exactly the same identification of pleasure with tickling as Descartes:

> Pleasure and pain accompany the operations of the senses. We feel pleasure when we taste good food, pain [*douleur*] when tasting bad food, and so on. This tickling of the senses [*chatouillement des sens*] that we find, for example, when tasting ripe fruit, sweet liquor, and other exquisite food, is called pleasure or sensuousness.[37]

35. Ibid.
36. Alexandre Matheron, "Descartes: la noblesse du chatouillement," *Dialectiques* 6 (1974) : 79–98.
37. *Traité de la connaissance*, 7.

We can see clearly that pleasure for Bossuet has a purely physiological cause—tickling. Pleasure results from the contact between external stimuli and the sensory organs. The pleasures of hearing a sermon, then, may be attributed to the delicately constructed organs of the ear and the prosodic contour of the preacher's voice. In other words, what makes for a persuasive sermon also makes for its transformation into a pleasurable, aesthetic object.

As we have seen, the ear—unlike the eye, which can be turned away or closed by shutting the eyelids—is always receptive, always open to the world. In addition, the aural "tickling" described by Bossuet is itself a purely physical operation that seemingly slips past the grasp of reason. Tone, pitch, inflexion, and rhythm affect the listener subtly and perhaps independently of the concept that is being linguistically conveyed. After all, hearing, as Bossuet writes in the *Traité de la connaissance*, depends on vibrations (*l'agitation*) of the air that in turn agitate the organs of the inner ear.[38] For Bossuet, the human voice may be a vehicle for thought, but it is an inadequate one insofar as it is freighted with vocal qualities (tone, pitch, rhythm, and so on) that affect the listener's disposition unconsciously. Thus the transformation of the sermon into a form of entertainment is not solely the fault of preachers who adorn their discourse with rhetorical ornaments or seek to accommodate the lax morality of their audience. A Bourdaloue, a Mascaron, or a Bossuet can delight an audience. It falls to the listener to carefully train his or her ear so as to override, as it were, the purely physiological "tickling" he or she feels. Left to his or her own devices, Bossuet suggests, the listener cannot help but be seduced by the pleasing sound of the preacher's voice and the rhythm of his oration.

Anticipating by three hundred years what Teresa Brennan calls "rhythmic entrainment," or the tendency of organisms to synchronize their movements in response to external rhythm, Bossuet asserts that human beings have a natural propensity to vibrate in sympathy with one another.[39] Bossuet illustrates this by way of a musical analogy. Baroque string instruments included both "plucked" strings, activated by the fingers, plectrum, or bow, and "sympathetic" or

38. Ibid., 104.
39. Teresa Brennan, *The Transmission of Affect* (Ithaca, N.Y.: Cornell University Press, 2004), 70.

"auxiliary" strings, which the musician "played" indirectly by virtue of sympathetic resonance.[40]

> This [that imitation is not the same as learning] appears clearly in song, and even in speech. Leave us to ourselves, and we will speak naturally in the same tone as our interlocutor. An echo does as much. Tune two lute strings to the same pitch and one sounds when the other is plucked. Something similar happens in us . . .[41]

The fact that human beings can hum a tune without following the musical score, can imitate the accents of others, and tend to speak in the same tone as those with whom they are conversing, results from a purely physical phenomenon. To reinforce his analogy, Bossuet compares this tendency to harmonize in sympathy with one another to an echo. The image of the echo, which repeats what has already been sounded, carries with it a negative connotation as a figure of sterility. It reproduces sound as if by reflex, calling to mind, perhaps, the "theatricality" of those congregants whose emotional outpouring during a sermon is due to "springs" and "artifices," "sterile and fruitless affections": a purely mechanical response to the preacher's impassioned speech.[42] Bossuet pursues the model of sympathetic resonance further, noting that the sympathetic response touches the very fibers of our being, affecting the body's motion as well as the quality of the voice:

> We are not only predisposed to sing in the same tone as those we listen to; our whole body moves in step, as long as we have a good ear; and this depends so little on our choice, that we must be forced to do otherwise, such is the proportion between the movements of the ear and these other parts.[43]

Bossuet complicates the model of sympathetic resonance by allowing for the possibility of synchronization by degree, where a human being responds to the rhythm of another human being who is responding to an external rhythm. This body-to-body synchronization is central to Brennan's theory of affective transfer, where affects move between bodies at an unconscious level; Bossuet cautions against the

---

40. The metaphor of the human body as a musical instrument is ancient, dating at least to Plato's *Phaedo* (85e-86b).
   41. *Traité de la connaissance*, 228.
   42. *Œuvres*, 132.
   43. *Traité*, 228–29.

danger of sympathy but also gestures toward its evangelical potential. While the "subtle contagion" of vice spreads indiscernibly, but always agreeably, from person to person, a wise maestro may be able to turn sympathetic resonance to his advantage.[44] In his *Fragments d'un discours sur la vie chrétienne* (Fragments of a Discourse on Christian Life), Bossuet employs the model of sympathetic resonance to illustrate the spread of religious fervor from one believer to another. Bossuet compares the human being to a string instrument awaiting divine activation. "Consider the strings of an instrument," he writes, "they are silent and immobile. When touched by a knowing hand, they receive its timing and rhythm, and even transfer it to the other strings."[45] Thus God's "knowing hand" plucks the strings of his faithful, whose religious zeal, devotion, and charity may in turn resonate with others.[46]

By adopting a mechanistic explanation of aural pleasure, Bossuet gives new life to the homiletic commonplace of "ticklish ears." For Bossuet, the ticklish ear is not simply a metaphor that illustrates congregants' desire to be flattered or to have the sermon accommodate one's way of life. Rather, the auricular "tickle" occasioned by the preacher's voice describes an automatic physiological process whereby the organs of the inner ear receive vibrations in the air. For Bossuet, as for Descartes, tickling (or *chatouillement*) is synonymous with pleasure understood as a sensation arising from a certain degree of force upon a delicate part of the human body. In this way, the pleasure derived from hearing a sermon may be entirely independent of its doctrinal content. Moreover, by considering the theatricality of the sermon within the context of homiletics and early modern audiology, we see that the ear, rather than the eye, is the primary organ through which preachers become "ministers of pleasure" and the pulpit a playhouse. As a consequence of Bossuet's mechanistic revision of the "ticklish ears" trope, it is not possible to blame the theatricalization of the pulpit on either the preacher or the congregation. The more melodious the priest's voice and the more carefully structured the sermon, the greater the sermon's rhetorical force, and the more likely it is to "tickle" the ears. Bossuet may have eschewed rhetorical

44. *Sermons*, 79.
45. *Œuvres* X, 484.
46. Bossuet is wary of the dangers of music, however, targeting Lully's enchanting melodies in particular. See *Maximes et réflexions sur la comédie* (1694), 7–8.

extravagance, relied on the authority of Biblical and patristic texts, and faithfully emulated Pauline simplicity; in his sermons on sacred eloquence he nonetheless voiced the concern that his listeners might forsake the message for the medium. We cannot today know the tone, pitch, and inflexions of Bossuet's voice, but his sermons, as Paul Valéry famously noted, constitute a full repository of literary forms that continue to fascinate, and perhaps even tickle.

FABIEN CAVAILLÉ

"Repaître nos yeux de ces vains spectacles": The Pleasures of the Spectator as the Pleasures of Eating in Pierre Nicole's *Traité de la Comédie* (1667)

In the *Première visionnaire*, written on December 31, 1665, the Jansenist Pierre Nicole violently attacked one of his opponents, Jean Desmarets de Saint-Sorlin, for having been a playwright and a novelist; he then pronounced a general condemnation of poets: "The novelist and playwright is a public poisoner, not of bodies, but of believers' souls, who should consider himself guilty of an infinite number of spiritual homicides that he has caused or may have caused by his pernicious writings."[1] A few days later, Racine publicly reacted against Nicole's attack: "You could have used kinder images than public poisoners and vile people polluting the Christians."[2] The *Visionnaires* controversy thus began with a particularly vehement simile equating playwrights with poisoners.

Although the metaphor of poison was common in polemics against the theater, Nicole's condemnation of playwrights as public poisoners is particularly brutal because it identifies writing with a real crime, which was punished by being burned at the stake, one of the major sources of anxiety during the reign of Louis XIV.[3] Indeed, by pouring venom into food, poisoners actively change nourishment into its opposite. They pervert healthy, refreshing dishes into unhealthy, destructive ones: what is supposed to strengthen life now carries death.

1. Pierre Nicole, *L'hérésie imaginaire* (1666), 168. My translations, here and throughout, unless indicated otherwise.
2. Jean Racine, *Lettre à l'auteur des hérésies imaginaires et des deux visionnaires* (1666) in Pierre Nicole, *Traité de la comédie*, ed. Laurent Thirouin (Paris: H. Champion, 1998), 226.
3. The metaphor of the public poisoner is more vivid and less stereotyped than the image of poison, which merely reiterates the Augustinian trope of theater as a plague or contagious disease.

YFS 130, *Guilty Pleasures: Theater, Piety, and Immorality in Seventeenth-Century France*, ed. Harris and Prest, © 2016 by Yale University.

At the same time, poisoners take advantage of the sensual pleasures of taste and smell to hide their deadly intention so that death has all the deceiving charms of life. The image of the playwright as a public poisoner reactivates and, at the same time, subverts the ancient analogy between poetry and cooking, between works of art and food.

One year later, in his *Traité de la comédie*, though he largely abandons the metaphor of poison, Nicole continues exploring the association between theater and healthy or unhealthy food, placing their relationship in a richer, more complex network of meanings. The obvious purpose of such an analogy is to depreciate the theater, making it an inferior pleasure that is too material, too corporeal to be appreciated by "honnêtes gens." The analogy between theater and food aims to make the reader feel guilty for attending such vile entertainment. But it cannot be reduced to a simple rhetorical tool for polemical purposes. The association between food and theater is too particular to Nicole's *Traité* to be innocuous. Although one can find, in some texts of the 1660s, a few images associating theater with poisoned food, these are rare and stereotyped. Only St. Francis of Sales developed in his *Introduction à la vie dévote* (1609) some comparisons between worldly pleasures, such as dances, music, and plays, and the corporeal pleasures of eating and drinking.[4] It is quite surprising, then, that Nicole should borrow such a parallel from someone who professes different views on religious matters. Unlike St. Francis of Sales, Nicole uses the analogy as a hermeneutic tool to reveal the guilty sensuality of theater and the exact nature of the spectator's pleasure. It helps him to deepen his moral analysis of the theatrical experience. The analogy between spectatorship and the ordinary and vital act of eating or feeding aims at crystallizing, in the reader's mind, and perhaps in Nicole's own mind, a large range of fears—from primal ones, of food poisoning or even ingestion, to religious horror or fascination for a

---

4. For example, "I am inclined to say about [dances] what doctors say of certain articles of food, such as mushrooms and the like—the best are not good for much; but if eat them you must, at least mind that they are properly cooked. So, if circumstances over which you have no control take you into such places, be watchful how you prepare to enter them. Let the dish be seasoned with moderation, dignity and good intentions. The doctors say (still referring to the mushrooms), eat sparingly of them, and that but seldom, for, however well dressed, an excess is harmful. So dance but little, and that rarely, my daughter, lest you run the risk of growing over fond of the amusement." St. Francis of Sales, *Introduction to the Devout Life* (no translator given, http://www.catholicspiritualdirection.org/devoutlife.pdf).

forbidden fruit or a sacrilegious Eucharist. To write about food in a treatise on theater is a meaningful choice when the author is a brilliant theologian.

GLUTTONY AND DISGUST: PARADOXES OF AN IMPOSSIBLE PLEASURE

Although the analogy has an obvious polemical purpose, it uses a subtle dialectic of corporeal appetites and sensual pleasures in order to prove that the theater entertains the body—not the mind, as its apologists claim—and responds to primary sensations (hunger, satiety, taste and smell, disgust) or faults (gluttony, voracity, intemperance, laziness). One might be surprised by the use of the verb *repaître*, which appears several times: " . . . how can we believe that we could feast [*repaître*] our eyes on those vain spectacles?"[5] As Furetière confirms, *repaître* is commonly used in classical French to express the idea of a satisfaction of the senses. Nonetheless, Furetière's illustrative examples suggest that the verb has pejorative connotations: it is clearly linked to gluttony ("He's a glutton who likes overeating [*repaître*] at another's expense")[6] or animality ("Our horses have to be fed [*repaître*]: they can't go further without eating").[7] *Repaître* suggests eating with voracity, like a beast. According to Nicole, the spectator does not simply watch the play, he devours it voraciously, and so figuratively commits the sin of gluttony. The theatrical experience is always perceived as a bodily excess: unable to moderate their greed for distraction, spectators cannot help but go beyond the limits of decency and sanity. Behind the spectator wasting his time at the theater and other worldly pleasures, Nicole imagines the figure of a monstrous eater who spends his life indulging in banquets:

> Just as it is certain that spending one's life eating all day long is highly criminal—what the Prophet condemns thus: *Vae qui consurgitis mane ad ebrietatem sectandam et potandum usque ad vesperam*—similarly one can easily see how spending all our life, which God has given us so that we can be His servants, in distractions, is to abuse it.[8]

5. *Traité de la comédie*, 110.
6. Antoine Furetière, "Repaître" in *Dictionnaire universel* (The Hague-Rotterdam: Arnout and Reinier Leers, 1690).
7. Ibid.
8. *Traité de la comédie*, 80.

Nicole makes a wider condemnation of all forms of entertainment by comparing the theater to the act of eating and to the social institution of the meal. Like in a banquet featuring dish after dish, the plays get lost among a larger list of worldly pleasures: "Their [worldly women's] life is a mere vicissitude of distractions. They spend it all in visits, games, balls, promenades, banquets, plays."[9] Nicole belittles even refined entertainments and relegates them to the vulgar, dissolute life of the greedy.

Nicole remarks that the gluttonous appetite for theater is never satisfied. Voracity for plays alters the spectator's soul just as an excessively heavy meal tires one's body. Images of drunkenness are used to show the results of this overindulgence in entertainment: "The mind is then entirely occupied by exterior objects and totally intoxicated [*enivré*] with the extravagances shown on stage."[10] Whereas the mind gets drunk, the body falls into lethargy: "When we feed on such vain worldly joys, our spiritual senses are numbed, and we are unable to enjoy [*goûter*] or listen to godly matters."[11] The theater weighs down the spectator's soul and mind and numbs his intellectual faculties. The dizziness and dullness that spectators experience after seeing a play are the signs of their own materiality, of the frailty and vanity of their being.

But Nicole sees another consequence of a voracious appetite for plays: spectators never gain any satisfaction from them, not because their desire is too great to be fulfilled, but because they never receive any pleasure from fulfilling their desire. In a remarkable and pessimistic contradiction, whereby gluttony produces only disgust, Nicole points out that no pleasure is to be found at the theater. Worldly women, in particular, are blamed for dissipating their life in worldly pleasures and being wearied by them: "Their boredom is a disgust resulting from satiety, similar to that resulting from an excess of food, and it must be cured by abstinence, and not by changing pleasures."[12] Spectators are led into a vicious circle in which they become more and more disgusted whenever they try to flee from this disgust. In Nicole's *Traité de la comédie*, there is no pleasure in theater—not even a guilty one—because disgust is the only effect plays have on the audience's feelings.

9. Ibid.
10. Ibid., 43.
11. Ibid., 95.
12. Ibid., 82.

DISTRACTION AND ASCETICISM:
HOW TO REFUTE THOMAS AQUINAS

However, Nicole's analogy is problematic: food provides life and strength to the body and so the parallel between theater and food could easily be turned into a positive one and plays might appear as essential as meals. In defense of the theater, an apologist would cite St. Thomas Aquinas, who, in his *Summa theologica*, demonstrates the vital utility of distractions (*ludus*), plays included. As Thomas Aquinas points out, it is not distraction itself that should be blamed, but its inappropriate or immoderate use.[13] Entertainment responds to a vital need: when, after a long stint working or studying, the mind becomes weary, it has to take rest and be refreshed, just like the body, and that refreshment implies pleasure.[14] For Thomas Aquinas, a man needs distractions and pleasures to be healthy; he has to cultivate the virtue of *eutrapelia*, the spirit of pleasantness or playfulness, which provides him with necessary respite from his spiritual preoccupations. Although there is no allusion to food in this famous demonstration, Thomas Aquinas shows that entertainments fulfill a vital need; it is not hard, then, to draw a positive analogy between theater and food. Nicole seems to be aware of this risk and, while he associates theater with meat (*viande*) throughout the *Traité de la comédie*, he sometimes tempers the analogy by noting that, unlike a real meal, the theater has no restorative power. According to Nicole, Thomas Aquinas is mistaken when he asserts that the pleasures of theater provide rest. Chapters XX to XXV wage war on Aquinas's apology of *eutrapelia*, which was often used to legitimize plays.

Rather than openly contesting Thomas Aquinas's notion that the mind and soul need rest after work, Nicole aims instead at redefining it. Nicole insists, far more than Thomas Aquinas does, on the practical purposes of entertainment: "Since entertainment [*divertissement*] is only useful in that it renews spiritual and bodily powers when work has weakened them, it is clear that one should only indulge in entertainment to the same extent that one may eat."[15] Nicole understands the idea of entertainment as a recreation—in the etymological sense—of the body or the mind: distraction serves to renew one's physical or intellectual strength; otherwise, it goes beyond its

13. St. Thomas Aquinas, *Summa theologica*, II^a II^{ae}, q. 168, art. 2 and 3.
14. Ibid., II^a II^{ae}, q. 168, art. 2 co.
15. *Traité de la comédie*, 78.

purpose and becomes sinful. The alimentary analogy at the end of the quotation insists on this utilitarian way of viewing entertainments and draws a clear line between what is good for the body or the mind and what should be considered as excess. To refute the idea of theater as legitimate recreation, Nicole uses the same arguments as the *Summa theologica* but diverts them from their original purpose.

Yet Nicole interprets Thomas Aquinas in a very restrictive and austere way. Redefining the nature of *divertissement* through the alimentary comparison, the Jansenist reduces the forms that entertainment can take. Although distraction is a vital need, it is also a rudimentary one, like eating. In order to be an appropriate restorative to man's strengths, distractions have to be natural—not sophisticated or artificial—like a simple and proper meal whose purpose is only to feed the body, not to satisfy sensual pleasures. A Christian cannot seek distractions that are not good for him, just as he cannot justify his gluttony by the natural need to eat: "As the need to eat does not make it acceptable for us to eat meats which only weaken the body, similarly the need for distraction cannot excuse those who seek distractions which only make their mind less apt for Christian living."[16] Obviously, the theater cannot be said to be a natural recreation, and that is why Nicole often associates plays with banquets or unhealthy food. Watching a play prevents the Christian from taking true rest; like a banquet, it weakens him instead of rejuvenating him. Consequently, it is easy to conclude that the theater is not the distraction Thomas Aquinas has in mind when he defends the *eutrapelia* provided by entertainment: "Theater cannot be seen as entertainment."[17] One might then ask what kind of *divertissement* Nicole does allow, since he does admit its necessity. Because all worldly pleasures are excluded, his definition becomes so limited that no form of entertainment remains. The only recreation that is natural and good for the body and the mind is inactivity.[18]

In refuting Thomas Aquinas by comparing distraction to eating, Nicole's alimentary imagery helps him define what a Christian way of life should be. If eating implies dietetics, a healthy use of aliments,

---

16. Ibid., 82.
17. Ibid.
18. "Satisfaction comes to the man who has worked well when he stops working and is distracted by what does not keep him busy." Ibid., 86.

there should be a dietetic use of distraction that ensures the health of souls. When Nicole draws his analogy, he also thinks about the rules of a virtuous life. Unlike St. Francis de Sales, he defines a virtuous life as an asceticism, a radical conversion—or a strict diet—that induces the believer to renounce all worldly pleasures. The comparison between distraction and eating helps the reader understand that giving up theater is a part of the Christian dietetics, so to speak, and a step toward spiritual asceticism. The only Christian recreations he is allowed to cultivate, those that give a true rest to his body and soul, are eating without greed and sleeping without laziness.

EYES, MOUTH, AND STOMACH: *LIBIDO SPECTANDI* AND THE FEAR OF INGESTION

In the *Traité de la comédie*, this asceticism is also described as a paradoxical conversion of our sight. As Laurent Thirouin remarks, the believer has to renounce theater and close his eyes to worldly vanities. Thirouin discerns in this endorsement of a salutary blindness the influence of Augustine of Hippo: theater is "the paroxysmal expression of *libido spectandi*, i.e. concupiscence of the eyes."[19] As in 1 John 2:16, Augustine distinguishes between three kinds of concupiscence.[20] All the corporeal pleasures (notably sex, food, and drink) involving the five senses belong to the *libido sentiendi* that induces sinners to seek *voluptas*. Greediness and drunkenness derive from this first type of concupiscence, which directly affects the body. However, the theater, like any other spectacle, is not a matter of *libido sentiendi* because it deals with the temptation of *curiositas* or *scientia*, the second type of concupiscence.[21] Although this art is based on the sense of sight, it affects the mind: sight is not used to take pleasure in material things, but rather to fulfill a desire for knowledge. Early modern Augustinian philosophers, like Jansenius and Nicole, repeat this distinction between theater and corporeal concupiscence.

A close reading of the *Traité de la comédie*, however, reveals Nicole's more complex view on *libido spectandi* because he sometimes describes sight in terms of eating (*repaître ses yeux*, "feasting one's

19. Laurent Thirouin, *L'aveuglement salutaire. Le réquisitoire contre le théâtre dans la France classique* (Paris: H. Champion, 1997), 240.
20. See Augustine of Hippo, *Confessions*, III, 8.
21. Ibid., X, 35.

eyes"). Seeing becomes an act of absorbing an external body through one's eyes, digesting it and incorporating it like food. Nicole imagines that the spectator's eyes devour plays as if the eyes were both mouth and stomach. The analogy between play and meal blurs the Augustinian distinction between the concupiscence of flesh (*libido sentiendi*) and the concupiscence of curiosity (*libido spectandi*): theater is the result of both desires, uniting *voluptas* and *curiositas*.

Nicole's spectator, and particularly the female spectator, is fed or filled by what s/he sees onstage:

> As only gallantry and extraordinary adventures are represented onstage, spectators' minds are imperceptibly permeated by a fanciful mood, filled with heroes and heroines; women, in particular, are so marked by this dream of this life that they can no longer bear the daily matters of their household.[22]

On a similar note Nicole writes:

> We always see a vivid representation of the passionate bond felt by men toward women, which cannot be blameless, and which will always result in women being filled with the pleasure of being loved and adored by men.[23]

Nicole pictures worldly women as greedy spectators overfilled with the pleasures they consume, and presents the female spectator as a living container, a stomach fed by the pleasure of attending the theater. More generally, the spectator is reduced to a desiring body whose appetite never ends and who is always seeking food. Although Nicole blames the theater for being a symptom of the human *libido spectandi*, at a deeper level he sees it as an expression of the body, not a sin of the mind, as if *voluptas* of the *libido sentendi* were hidden in *curiositas*.

These images of ingestion also help us to understand how Nicole perceives the activity of seeing plays. Instead of being a cognitive process involving imagination and reason, visual perception becomes a movement from the exterior to the interior of the spectator's body that

---

22. *Traité de la comédie*, 84.
23. Ibid., 57. See also: "It is enough to oblige those who care somewhat for their salvation to avoid Plays, Balls, and Novels, whereby, more than by anything else in the world, the soul is expelled and one is made unable to turn to God and is instead filled with vain ghosts. The prayers that you make when you leave such spectacles are strange indeed because your head is full of all the extravagances you have just seen." Ibid., 90.

keeps him totally passive. This understanding of sight is confirmed by other expressions Nicole uses to describe cognitive aspects of the spectator's activity: "The more they [playwrights] color these vices with an image of grandeur and generosity, the more dangerous they make them, the more able to enter the most well-born souls."[24] The process of watching is limited to a sensual impression, a movement that goes from the outside to the inside of the subject. One might say that this has been the traditional interpretation of visual perception since Aristotle: images of the world enter the subject's imagination and provide the mind with information. In Nicole's presentation, however, the activity of seeing appears more like an invasion of the body from the outside that threatens the soul and blurs the limits with the inside and destroys the subject's integrity. The spectator is invaded by the play that he watches greedily, and he incorporates an alien element that infects him like poisonous food. Nicole's hatred of the theater seems to be provoked by a very primal (and perhaps unconscious) fear of ingestion and of a weak, passive body threatened by the very thing that is supposed to keep it alive.

A HOLY AVERSION: THE THEATER AND THE EUCHARISTIC MYSTERY

It is not surprising that, in the last sentence of his treatise, Nicole invites the reader to be horrified by the theater: "How can we believe that we could feast our eyes on those vain spectacles, and draw satisfaction from that which we should hate and which should horrify us?"[25] At the end of the *Traité de la comédie*, this horror is provoked not only by violent passions performed on stage, but, more fundamentally, by theater itself. The analogy Nicole draws between watching a play and eating helps us to understand why Nicole feels such horror for this art.

In his treatise, Nicole opposes two sorts of food: the poisoned variety (that is, all worldly pleasures) and the spiritual variety (those that feed the soul of the good Christian). God, too, offers something to eat to his believer: religion is a matter of food, which is why the author uses alimentary metaphors to describe the benefits of a Christian life: these benefits are the "holy delicacies [*saintes délices*] that raise

---

24. Ibid., 63.
25. *Traité de la comédie*, 112.

Christian souls away from this worldly desert."[26] Good Christians cannot be satisfied by the worldly pleasures of theater:

> All these distractions, which are so agreeable to worldly people, are but tasteless meat to them, they will not have it, because nothing can be seen there but emptiness, nothingness, vanity and folly, and no-where appears the salt of truth and wisdom. Thus can they say, along with Job, that they will not taste it: *An poterit comedi insulsum quod non est sale conditum?* Who could eat that unsalted meat?[27]

Alimentary metaphors help Nicole to praise religious qualities and to condemn the pleasures of theater. To the good taste (*bon goût*) of the worldly (*les gens du monde*), he opposes the spiritual taste of devout believers who, like King David, can "taste [*goûter*] the sweet-ness of divine law."[28] Through those comparisons, Nicole invokes the greatest authority he can find: the Bible, which refers to a wide range of food, from the forbidden fruit in the Garden of Eden to the manna sent down to the Israelites and the Last Supper. Indeed, the Catholic liturgy is based on a rite of *theophagia*, a sort of sacred can-nibalism: the believer eats the host that has become God, thanks to the ritual performed by the priest. In the *Traité de la comédie*, God feeds the Christian in two different ways: first, with the food of his Word (the prophet Jeremiah had a "spiritual taste [*goût spirituel*] for His word"[29]); then, with the body of his Son (the Christian is a "son of God . . . a member of the body of Christ, illuminated by His truth, enriched by His grace, nourished [*nourri*] by His body."[30] As Nicole reminds us, the only appropriate food to feed men both in a spiritual and material way is the Eucharist.

It is probably no coincidence that, in the same year that Nicole published his *Traité de la comédie*, he also fought against Protestant ministers in the never-ending controversy of the Eucharist. From 1664 to 1674, he wrote the *Perpétuité de la foi de l'Église catholique touchant l'Eucharistie* with Antoine Arnauld.[31] This lengthy treatise

26. Ibid., 92.
27. Ibid., 94.
28. Ibid.
29. Ibid.
30. Ibid., 104
31. See Nicole and Antoine Arnauld, *Perpétuité de la foi de l'Église catholique touchant l'Eucharistie, défendue contre le livre du sieur Claude, ministre de Charen-ton, par le sieur Arnauld et Nicole* (Paris: C. Savreux, 1669, 1672, 1674). A short ver-sion of this book was first published in 1664.

aimed to prove, once again, the rightness of the Catholic conception of the Eucharist and the reality of Transubstantiation during the
mass. In the meantime, Arnauld and Nicole were also working on
an extended version of *La logique ou l'art de penser* in order to demonstrate the peculiarity of the Eucharist as a sign. Furthermore, the
Jansenist nuns of Port-Royal were cultivating a special reverence for
the Eucharist. As with other trends in Tridentine Catholicism, the
Jansenists were fascinated by the idea that the divine Presence was
embodied in a piece of bread. Frank Lestringant points out: "Passion
and hunger for the Host are but the other side of that holy horror
which so deeply disgusts the Protestants."[32] This passion for the Eucharist helps one understand why the image of consuming theater is
so repugnant to Nicole.

For Nicole, theater appears as an inversion or, at least, as a deg-
radation of the spiritual food represented by the Eucharist. In chapter XXVII of his Treatise, which opposes the worldly pleasures of the
theater to the spiritual delights delivered by God, Nicole compares
distractions to a tasteless meat and to green grapes; they are imper-
fect versions of bread and wine, the Eucharistic species. This chapter implies that theater leads the Christian to a false communion,
which provokes anxiety of a special kind in Nicole's conscience, as if
the theater troubled his conception of the Eucharistic mystery. This
anxiety about the Eucharist may be the core of the horror that strikes
the Jansenist. Indeed, the theater is a matter of body and word, it
stages the attribution of an identity to a body by words; it deals with
physical presence, reference, and language. Even though theatrical
incarnation is not parallel to the divine Presence embodied in the
host, the process of fiction peculiar to theater threatens the mystery
of transubstantiation by casting the shadow of representation on it.
What if the host were just a piece of bread playing the part of the body
of Christ, like a prop? What if Calvin was right and the Eucharist was
only a figure of the body and the blood, deprived of the presence of
God? Nicole and Arnauld's purpose, in the *Perpétuité de la foi* and in
the *Logique*, is to maintain the divine Presence in the host: "Unlike
the remote God of the Calvinists, whose body has withdrawn into the
sky, Pascal's hidden God, the God of Port-Royal is really present in
the world, and this reassuring presence has to be of the flesh. It hides

32. Frank Lestringant, *Une sainte horreur. Voyage en Eucharistie* (Geneva: Librairie Droz, 2012), 322.

under the veil of flour and dough intended for our weakness."[33] According to Catholic theology, the Host is more than bread; it is not a representation or a symbol.

Nicole opens his *Traité de la comédie* with a definition of theater: "A play, they say, is a representation of actions and words as if they were present."[34] He concludes his book by repeating this assertion: "For if every temporal thing is but a figure and a shadow deprived of substance, we may say that plays are shadows of shadows and figures of figures."[35] Inspired by Plato's condemnation of theater, Nicole insists on the theater's representative nature: theater shows Christians signs based on an incarnation that does not imply the presence of things or beings; actions performed on stage and words pronounced by actors both lack efficacy; they are mere representations of words and actions. Theater deals with figures and, as the *Traité de la comédie* describes it, spectators eat those figures during the performance, just as Protestants eat and drink the sacred species, figures of the body and of the blood of Jesus Christ, as they see it. Theater is built on a semiotic regime that disturbs Nicole because it confronts spectators with a world of signs deprived of the presence of God.

All in all, the analogy between the pleasures of theater and the pleasures of eating, and between plays and food, are symptoms of a larger concern that goes beyond the question of the theater. It reveals a double problem concerning the Eucharist. The theater deals with a conception of signs that troubles the Catholic reading of this mystery. A horror of theatrical representation also seems to be the mirror and, perhaps, as Lestringant suggests, the unconscious transfer of the holy aversion (*sainte horreur*) that Protestants feel toward the sacred cannibalism of the Catholic mass.[36] Even though Port-Royal firmly resists the removal of God from the world as implied by the Protestant conception of the Eucharist, the Eucharist may have damaged and troubled Nicole's conscience. Is theater the real problem for him after all? Behind these plays greedily consumed by male and female spectators, one can make out the specter of those religions that only see signs and figures of God in the world. In Nicole's eyes, the theater might be a mask behind which the heresies of Protestantism hide.

---

33. Ibid., 337.
34. *Traité de la comédie*, 34.
35. Ibid., 108.
36. Lestringant, *Une sainte horreur*, passim.

Contributors

Hall Bjørnstad is Associate Professor of French Literature at Indiana University, Bloomington. He is the author of *Créature sans créateur: Pour une anthropologie baroque dans les "Pensées" de Pascal* (PU Laval, 2010; Hermann, 2013), the editor of *Borrowed Feathers: Plagiarism and the Limits of Imitation in Early Modern Europe* (Unipub, Oslo, 2008), and, with Katherine Ibbett, co-editor of volume 124 of *Yale French Studies*, "Walter Benjamin's Hypothetical French *Trauerspiel*" (2013).

Michael Call is Associate Professor at Brigham Young University. His publications include *The Would-Be Author: Molière and the Comedy of Print* (Purdue University Press, 2015) and several articles examining the notion of theatrical authorship in seventeenth-century France.

Fabien Cavaillé is *maître de conférences* at the Université de Caen-Basse Normandie. He has edited several plays by Alexandre Hardy and published articles on staging violence and the use of pathos, the civic use of theater and festivals, and spectatorship and theater building during the seventeenth and eighteenth centuries. His monograph *Alexandre Hardy et le théâtre de ville français au début du XVIIe siècle* is forthcoming from Garnier. He is currently working on love, nature and the Golden Age in French pastorals and festivals.

Perry Gethner is Regents Professor, Norris Professor of French and Head of the Department of Foreign Languages at Oklahoma State University. Among his works are numerous critical editions and translations of Rotrou, Mairet, Du Ryer, Thomas Corneille, Voltaire, and women playwrights of the seventeenth and eighteenth

YFS 130, *Guilty Pleasures: Theater, Piety, and Immorality in Seventeenth-Century France,* ed. Harris and Prest, © 2016 by Yale University.

centuries. He has also published articles dealing with various aspects of French drama and opera in the early modern period.

NICHOLAS HAMMOND is Professor of Early Modern French Literature and Culture at Cambridge University. In addition to writing several books on subjects ranging from Blaise Pascal and Port-Royal to seventeenth-century gossip and sexuality, he co-edited the *Cambridge History of French Literature* and edited the complete poetry of the libertine poet Saint-Pavin. Currently he is working on a large-scale project, Parisian Soundscapes (*www.parisian soundscapes.org*), which involves the recovery and performance of street songs.

JOSEPH HARRIS is Reader in Early Modern Studies at Royal Holloway, University of London. He has published widely on such themes as gender, laughter, and spectatorship in seventeenth- and eighteenth-century French literature (especially drama), and is the author of *Hidden Agendas: Cross-Dressing in Seventeenth-Century France* (Tübingen: Narr, 2005) and *Inventing the Spectator: Subjectivity and the Theatrical Experience in Early Modern France* (Oxford: OUP, 2014). He is currently writing a monograph on death in the works of Pierre Corneille.

THERESA VARNEY KENNEDY is Associate Professor of French at Baylor University where she has been teaching since 2008. Her primary research interests are in seventeenth-century theater, female playwrights, and the representation of women in classical French theater and beyond. She has published articles in *The French Review, Papers on French Seventeenth-Century Literature, Cahiers du Dix-Septième, Women in French Studies*, and *Neophilologus*. Classiques Garnier recently published her critical edition of Madame de Maintenon's proverbs, co-authored with Perry Gethner.

JULIA PREST is Reader in Early Modern French at the University of St Andrews. She has published widely on various aspects of early modern drama. Her publications include *Theatre under Louis XIV: Cross-Casting and the Performance of Gender in Drama, Ballet and Opera* (Palgrave, 2006; 2013) and *Controversy in French Drama: Molière's* Tartuffe *and the Struggle for Influence* (Palgrave, 2014; 2016). She is currently working on the social politics of the theatre in eighteenth-century Saint-Domingue (now Haiti).

CHRISTOPHER SEMK is Assistant Professor of French at Yale University. His book *Playing the Martyr: Theater and Theology in Early Modern France* will be published by Bucknell University. He is currently working on a book that examines theology and style in Bossuet's sermons.

EMILIA WILTON-GODBERFFORDE is Lecturer in French at the Open University. She has taught French at the University of Cambridge and was a research fellow at Clare Hall, Cambridge between 2012 and 2014. She is currently preparing her doctoral thesis, "Mendacity and the Figure of the Liar in Seventeenth-Century French Comedy," for publication as a monograph. She has published articles on Molière, Rotrou, and Tristan L'Hermite, and is co-authoring a textbook on translation in French for Routledge.

Yale French Studies is the oldest English-language journal in the United States devoted to French and Francophone literature and culture. Each volume is conceived and organized by a guest editor or editors around a particular theme or author. Interdisciplinary approaches are particularly welcome, as are contributions from scholars and writers from around the world. Recent volumes have been devoted to a wide variety of subjects, among them: Levinas; Perec; Paulhan; Haiti; Belgium; Crime Fiction; Surrealism; Material Culture in Medieval and Renaissance France; and French Education.

Yale French Studies is published twice yearly by Yale University Press (yalebooks.com) and may be accessed on JSTOR (jstor.org).

For information on how to submit a proposal for a volume of *Yale French Studies*, visit yale.edu/french and click "Yale French Studies."